NO SUCH

03

NO SUCH THING AS SOCIETY?

Individualism and Community

John Kingdom

Open University Press
Buckingham • Philadelphia

Open University Press
Celtic Court
22 Ballmoor
Buckingham
MK18 1XW

and
1900 Frost Road, Suite 101
Bristol, PA 19007, USA

First Published 1992

A catalogue record of this book is available from the British Library

Library of Congress Cataloging-in-Publication Data

Kingdom, J. E., 1939–
    No such thing as society? : individualism and community/John Kingdom.
       p.   cm.
    Includes bibliographical references and index.
    ISBN 0-335-09727-8 — ISBN 0-335-09726-X (pbk.)
    1. Individualism.   2. Collectivism.   3. Community.
  4. Citizenship.   I. Title.
  JC571.K53   1992
  320.5'12—dc20   91-46208
                                                           CIP

Typeset by Colset Private Limited, Singapore
Printed in Great Britain by St Edmundsbury Press Limited
Bury St Edmunds, Suffolk

To my mother

CONTENTS

PREFACE

Aristotle's celebrated aphorism that people were essentially political animals contained a note of authenticity which has resounded throughout the ages. The solitary life was one doomed forever to fall short of the good life seen by the ancient Greeks as the self-evident quest of reasoning beings; the one who denied the communal nature of existence was either a beast or a god. Yet in the 1980s, when the ideologues of the New Right captured the heights of British politics, this message was challenged at its very heart. Indeed, in praising a new form of sovereignty, that of the lone consumer haughtily ruling his court, the market-place, they actually seemed to offer people god-like status. Or were they making them beasts? Were they sacrificing that most singular human inheritance, reason, for the right to fight tooth and claw in an internecine struggle for nothing more than an animal satisfaction of the appetites? There can be no doubt that the era bequeathed some serious questions to the 1990s.

The need for questioning was made more insistent by the fact that the promise of economic abundance from the New Right appeared hollow. After an experiment lasting over thirteen years the strategy had demonstrably failed, even by its own uncomplicated materialistic standards. If communism was held to be the god that failed the left, so individualism had betrayed the New Right (Piachaud 1991: 205). One response to the failure was the frenzied butchering of the chatelaine of the fortress of New Right certainties, the replacement of Margaret Thatcher by John Major signalling that the nostrums were to be reappraised.

Yet the 1992 general election called in the deepest recession of the post-war era, revealed the deep-seated success of the Thatcher project. The opinion pollsters misread the trends, to emerge with more egg on their faces than had landed on the politicians' coats during the campaign. The late swing towards the Conservatives, operating below the psephological radar, which has become a regular feature of British general elections, revealed the potency of the secret ballot in a new way. While telling the pollsters they were uneasy with the values of individualism, in the closet of the polling booth people performed the solitary rites of self-love.

Yet, despite the triumphalism of Essex Man and the tabloid press, Conservative democrats could not in their sober moments regard a fourth term as entirely good for any democracy, particularly when that party continued to enjoy the support of only 42 per cent of those voting. Moreover, the slim 21-seat margin of the new government could not indefinitely withstand erosion by by-elections. John Major spoke of a classless society and the preservation of the NHS, making his cry 'welfare through wealth'. On the other side of the political divide the talk was of alliances, deals and electoral reform. Martin Jacques asserted that the time had come 'for the historic split in the centre-left between Labour and the Liberal Democrats to be seriously confronted' (*Observer*, 12 April 1992).

Hence, despite the seemingly impregnable position of the Conservative Party, Britain was at a crossroads. If the 1980s had been a decade of unremitting action, where the doers were exalted above the questioners, the 1990s demanded more talking and a more critical reappraisal of the values promoted during the previous thirteen years. The issues were not mere party advantage; they were about human nature, the meaning of society, the nature of the state, the modes of producing and distributing the materials sustaining life, the ecological balance between the human species and nature and, ultimately, the morality which determines the way we live together.

Various people deserve my thanks in the preparation of this essay. Ray Cunningham of the Open University Press made the original suggestion following a conference paper I delivered at a Public Administration conference at York University at the invitation of Professor Bob Haigh and Dave Morris. Richard Baggaley took over the editorial role at the Open University Press during the project and has made many thoughtful suggestions. My colleagues Janet Marrison, Malcolm Stevens and Ann Wall kindly read an earlier draft of the manuscript, offering considerable help and encouragement in many ways. Finally, as always, I owe an enormous debt to my wife Ann for her extremely meticulous, yet creative, copy-editing and the compilation of an excellent index. Needless to say, the faults and idiosyncrasies remain mine and mine alone.

1 THE MASTURBATORY SOCIETY

When Margaret Thatcher made her imperious declaration that 'there is no such thing as society' she captured the essence of a political mission. As with most Thatcher revelations, the pronouncement was not original, being one of the sentiments of a prince of individualism, the eccentric nineteenth-century egomaniac, Jeremy Bentham (1970: 12), for whom society was but a 'fictitious body'. Thatcher challenged the notion that Britain could be a community; at a stroke people were to be relieved of any responsibility for one another, the biblical maxim 'love thy neighbour' exposed as ill-conceived post-war funk.

Although the era saw legislation specifically discouraging homosexual relationships, Thatcherite doctrines offered little encouragement to love anyone at all – anyone, that is, other than oneself. This was to be the masturbatory society, offering a solitary view of fulfilment, free of the complications arising from tiresome moral demands by others. Defoe did not report how Robinson Crusoe satisfied his urges, either before or after encountering Man Friday, but he was to become the icon of an age, that of the new individualist. This was to be the era of casino capitalism. People would relate to one another like players at the roulette table; the winners would be applauded while the losers could quietly place the loaded pistol in their mouths.

The individualist credo cast a monstrous and intimidating shadow over political debate throughout the 1980s and is set to continue into the 1990s. Yet like any shadow it is devoid of substance, enlarged to frightening proportions by a white light of strident rhetoric. At the source of the shadow we discover a flimsy pattern of paper cut-out ideas.

Thatcherism: the march of the new individualists

By the end of the 1980s few in Britain were unfamiliar with the credo which took the very name of its crusading virago: Thatcherism, a panacea to remedy all manner of maladies and restore Britain's position in the world. Precise definition remained elusive, scholars portraying it variously and debating its nuances with flattering intensity (Jessop *et al.* 1988: 5–21). Essentially it was an unstable amalgam of economic liberalism, monetarism, anti-corporatism, authoritarianism and populism (Benyon 1989: 170–1). Although for some it was little more than a crude, naive radicalism (Hindess 1987: 152), it demanded to be taken seriously, for by 1980 it was regarded for all practical purposes as Conservatism itself (Young 1990: 236). The Thatcherite agenda entailed nothing less than the death of what she herself termed 'socialism', and what others termed 'social democracy', as the price of national economic revival. The assault was to be directed at both the institutions and the culture which was held to sustain them.

Eventually Thatcher was to depart, a truly classical tragic heroine destroyed by a fatal flaw which, with majestic irony, was the very egoism she had so triumphally proclaimed. Unable to see any way but hers, beset by rampant xenophobia, and clinging to a system of taxation which betrayed an unconscionable meanness of spirit, she was finally alone when she needed friends. What had been achieved? After an era of masochistically imbibing her patent brand of socioeconomic castor oil, it was painfully apparent that the ailing country had not risen from its sick-bed. As government rhetoric had spoken of a return to Victorian values, so the economy languished like a Pre-Raphaelite lady afflicted by the vapours.

The economy had gone through a traumatic process of de-industrialization, with imports from Europe, the US and Japan crowding out domestic production. The proportion of investment going abroad increased dramatically with the lifting of exchange controls, resulting in job losses in Britain even though investors could themselves grow fat. Such jobs as were created at home were generally in the service industries, many of the services being for the wealthy. In addition, spending on the basic infrastructure fell while European competitors were stepping theirs up. Living standards also declined to a level such that 'only Eire, Portugal and Greece stand lower in the league table' (Barratt Brown 1991: 5–7). On Thatcher's final Commons appearance as Prime Minister, Labour's Neil Kinnock chided her with having begun and ended her reign in deep recession with a 'miracle' in the middle.

However, the death of social democracy appeared to have been a more successful project, much of the state resembling a smoking site after a visit by the Luftwaffe. Social services, education and health care were in a state of crisis. Tax cuts for the wealthy, paid for by privatizing national assets, cuts in social provision and a bonanza of North Sea oil, resulted in the top tenth of the population doubling their real incomes while the bottom tenth grew poorer (Barratt Brown 1991: 6). The third Thatcher general election victory had seen her announcing, with taunting braggadocio, a mission accomplished, and that it was she herself who had done the bloody deed. Not only had she killed socialism, she had 'buried' it. Certainly the institutions of the post-war welfare state had been vandalized and rude New Right grafitti scrawled over its walls. Even more astonishing was the fact that this could be seen as something to boast about, for it was little more than 40 years since Britain had, in a resounding landslide, rejected Churchill, a legendary statesman and war leader, in favour of Attlee, who looked and sounded more like a clerk in the Ministry of Social Security than a world statesman of a new era. The post-war years had seen intense pride in the British welfare state and the National Health Service, its greatest monument, was held up as a model for the world. The institutions of British social democracy had certainly been assaulted; so had the minds of its people. How could all this have happened with so little opposition?

Do ideas matter?

The extent to which ideas influence political events is a matter of dispute. Only rarely do thinkers enjoy the exhilaration of seeing their thoughts clothed in the flesh of action. Yet ideas permeate the cultural atmosphere, entering our minds through intellectual osmosis to influence our attitudes on what is right or wrong, natural or unnatural (Gramsci 1971). One does not have to have read Charles Darwin or J. S. Mill to reflect their thoughts. Macho men of affairs might wish to deny any wimpish propensity towards philosophical rumination, but Keynes famously remarked that those 'who believe themselves to be quite exempt from any intellectual influences are usually the slaves of some defunct economist' (Keynes 1936: 383). When despots hear voices they are usually receiving an echo of some cloistered academic ringing down the years.

Yet the early post-war decades of British politics were particularly tranquil on the ideological front; it was not so much that thoughts did not exist, but that people found little to argue about. This was a consensus era, and Daniel Bell (1960) earned celebrity by coining the term 'the end of ideology' to capture this new *Zeitgeist*. However, the Thatcher era was to thrust ideology to the fore in a provocative manner. Margaret Thatcher herself rejoiced in the sobriquet 'Iron Lady', memorably proclaiming in advertising jinglese: 'This lady's not for turning'. Although throughout her career it was not in the lady's nature to come up with thoughts of her own (Young 1990), interest in ideas was signalled through assiduous courtship of right-wing academics and polemicists such as monetarist guru Milton Friedman. She also encouraged the efforts of right-wing think-tanks such as the Centre for Policy Studies (set up by Sir Keith Joseph when he had despaired of his political colleagues for ideas), the Adam Smith Institute, the Institute of Economic Affairs and the Salisbury Group. In addition she enlarged the Prime Ministers' Policy Unit (created by Harold Wilson) and elevated the role of personal advisers such as Alan Walters, whose cuckoo-like presence led to the petulant flight from the cabinet nest of Chancellor Nigel Lawson in 1989.

The ideological thrust of the approach was apparent in the way that policies were pushed well beyond their pragmatic utility. Privatization, for example, would not have been pursued so far (from British Airways to refuse collection) without an undeviating general commitment to the virtues of the market (Hindess 1987: 152). Indeed, as she lived so she died, for it was her unyielding adherence to anti-European and pro-poll-tax sentiments that roused in others an equally compelling conviction that the style had passed its electoral sell-by date.

Yet for Thatcher and many in her train the discovery of New Right ideology was perhaps that of Molière's Monsieur Jordain in *Le Bourgeois Gentilhomme*, who was so pleasurably astonished to learn from his teacher that in his mundane utterances he had been speaking prose for over 40 years. *La bourgeoise gentilledame* of Finchley learned that her tortuous enunciation had for long been the prose of the New Right philosophers; she had learned it on her father's knee above the Grantham grocer's shop which was to enter the world of constitutional fable. The term 'New Right' became part of everyday political jargon, journalists and politicians proclaiming themselves to be, or not to be, devotees of its prescriptions and nostrums. Moreover, ordinary folk themselves discovered that, in the privacy of their parlours, bars and clubs, they too, like Margaret Thatcher and Monsieur Jordain, had been speaking with the golden tongues of philosophers. What is the New Right?

The New Right

In fact much of the diverse baggage labelled 'New Right' looked much like the old in Dayglo wrapping. Sometimes the New Right luminaries basked in the title 'neo-liberal', but this label is hardly justified in view of the sophisticated and subtle thoughts of other liberals such as Rawls (1973) and Dworkin (1984), who have developed the humane and tolerant tradition begun by J. S. Mill. The intellectual axioms of the New Right came, with little restoration, from the seventeenth to early nineteenth centuries. Economically there was the work of Friedrich Hayek and Milton Friedman, who had acted throughout the post-war consensus era as curators of the museum of classical economics and liberalism. The basic free-market ideas of Adam Smith, David Ricardo and Thomas Malthus were reverently disinterred, dusted and given a suitable gloss for the new era. The idea of tradition was also venerated, but only selectively. The traditions of liberalism were held to be hallowed, and to have been eroded by the post-war welfare state, but the traditions of democracy received a less favourable appraisal. Leading Conservative politician Lord Hailsham agonized in his BBC Reith lectures over the terrifying threat of 'elective dictatorship' within the once-liberal constitution. In addition, a complex body of thought termed 'public choice theory', hailing from the US, applied the techniques of economics to the analysis of politics.

There was also a resurgence of far-right-think promoted by British academics such as Roger Scruton, which revived the more mystical Burkean reasoning of conservatism (based on the belief that the status quo should be respected on the grounds that it was the embodiment of the accumulated wisdom of the ages), encouraging a range of backwards-looking policies such as repatriation of immigrants (mainly black ones), male domination within society and the family, a strong British presence in the world, militarism, Queen-and-country patriotism, hanging, and a generally more authoritarian style of government. Amongst this *petit bourgeois* prejudice could be found the prose that many had been speaking. The new rhetoric adorned it with a new respectability.

Essentially the various strands of the New Right tapestry added up to a reversal of the collectivist tendencies which had characterized post-war Britain; faith in individualism was reasserted. Where the New Right parted company from the old was in the idea of reason. The New Right thinkers were to go further than the Burkean appeal to tradition, basing their case on social science research, mathematical techniques and clever utilitarian argument. However, in their hearts they remained in a nineteenth-century ethical time warp.

The perils of revisionism

The impact of the Thatcherite project was evident in the response of the political opposition. At the risk of rather saucy transvestitism, her garments were seized upon as hand-me-downs, examined, taken in here and let down there, and worn sometimes sheepishly and sometimes with aplomb.

Initially this was not so. In the early 1980s the Labour Party was riven by internal dissent as the left opposed the New Right and political scientists spoke of the end of consensus. Faced with a classic example of the exit, voice or loyalty trichotomy (Hirschman 1970), all three alternatives were taken by party members. Most theatrical were the exiters; despairing of the rising tide of the left, their actions were calculated to 'break the mould' of British party politics. Shirley Williams, Roy Jenkins, William Rogers and David Owen formed an original 'Gang of Four' and, by the end of 1981, the new Social Democratic Party, growing like the rib plucked from Adam's breast, could boast a membership of 27 ex-Labour MPs (and a lone Conservative). Their policy talk was of moderation and the middle way and their political strategy spoke of proportional representation and coalition government.

The voice option was chosen by the left, who used it megaphonically, their main clarion being Tony Benn. Applying Newton's law of motion, they sought to pose against Thatcher an equal and opposite force, aiming to retreat from the post-war consensus position as far in the opposite direction. Gaining ascendancy within the party they promoted changes in the leadership selection, giving more power to the extra-parliamentary party and securing the compulsory reselection of MPs by the constituency rank and file. Within local government the New Urban Left rose to compensate for loss of parliamentary power, fighting for socialism in the town halls and even in the streets (Boddy and Fudge 1984). Yet events were to be cruel. In the 1983 general election the party flew its most clearly left-wing manifesto (derided by moderate Peter Shore as 'the longest suicide note in history'), but was never to know the effect, since the 'Falklands factor' raised Thatcher to impregnable great-war-leader status.

Electoral nemesis lent little credibility to the claim that the people of Britain were yearning for true socialism and, within the party, those choosing loyalty to the traditions of social democracy and 'Labourism' were to reassert themselves under the leadership of Neil Kinnock, who had been chosen, ironically, under the new system. Acceptance of the Thatcherite agenda was dignified as 'new realism', to be justified variously on the grounds of political expediency (rather like the Conservatives in the 1950s) or genuine admiration of parts of the Thatcher programme. Yet the revisionist tone itself legitimated the ideals of Thatcherism. Rather than returning to Fabian-style policy traditions, Labour seemed willing to seek office at almost any cost. Party leaders even began to look like Thatcherites, with sharp suits, streamlined briefcases and Filofaxes. Much of the new realism condones essentially individualist values and the party's new men, of moderate persuasion and silken tongues, were to talk easily the language of 'freedom', 'choice' and the 'market'. It seemed that socialism could live only by not being socialist; it was not only

Thatcherites at the graveside as the earth was shovelled over the coffin of social democracy.

The new individualists

The impulse behind both the Thatcher assault and the revisionist resonances in the political opposition was that individualism is the most desirable basis for behaviour in society. The justifications are both psychological and utilitarian. Psychologically it is argued that it is natural, that each person is governed by an unquenchable instinct for self-preservation, a desire to look out for the self, to pull up the ladder and 'never do owt for nowt, unless thee does it for thissen'. Any social system that does not take this hard fact into account will be naively utopian and doomed to failure. The utilitarian argument goes further, insisting that if each person acts according to naked self-interest, the end result will be the best for society. Life is a great game of cricket where, if each player scores as many runs as possible, the team will triumph.

Individualism argues that each person has an identity and character entirely independent of social formations. It is possible to fully comprehend the nature of a person without reference to society. Institutions such as the law courts, the Church and the state have no reality beyond their members and, consequently, have no constitutive part in the nature of the individual. Using this reasoning, the state is nothing more than a set of constraints on individuals.

The fragile community

The ideological counterpoise to individualism is collectivism, a term used rather loosely in practice, but essentially taking the whole society, rather than the individual, as the ethical starting point. In this view the individual is socially constructed; everyone is born into a social group which makes them what they are. Communal ethics require individuals to place the general good before self-interest – the polar opposite of the individualist ethic. It implies love and regard for one's fellows, while the individualist finds nobility in the idea of selfishness.

Yet in modern times the community is never safe. As in classical tragedy, it appears to harbour the seeds of its own destruction stemming from the idea of reason, the conviction that the head should rule the heart in the search for the good life. Frazer revealed how, within primitive society, mysticism and magic conjured up by the imagination emerge to give a sense of increased strength against the vagaries of nature (Frazer 1925: 217). From this evolves science, the quest for knowledge and a faith in reason, the sweet taste of the forbidden fruit. Today rationality is consecrated as a supreme value in an industrial society, its legitimacy lying in its power to satisfy the interests of all members (Gamble 1981: 228). But there are monstrous risks; only the individual can bite the apple and reason can displace the social context and elevate the sense of self. The thinking individual seeks emancipation from the conservative norms of the community to question, challenge and discover new possibilities, even to threaten the community itself. Along with the striking potential for advance come new opportunites for evil in the form of egoism, greed, violence, destruction, loneliness and guilt. As individualism becomes a cult, an end in itself, it seeks its justification from philosophers, so that even the religion that preaches love of one's neighbour becomes a quest for personal salvation.

It has been argued that the rise of collectivism seen in 'the extension of the role of government at all levels' has been the most salient feature of British political life since the nineteenth century (Greenleaf 1983). This of course is indisputable in institutional terms, but the argument of this essay is that institutional collectivism was not matched by the emergence of a communal spirit, and for this reason the post-war social democratic state was incomplete and vulnerable. British political culture remained ingrained with a particular form of individualism which became increasingly out of kilter with the needs of the contemporary world. The New Right, with its deification of the individual, found this fecund soil in which to thrust its roots in the 1980s. Yet the thinking is deeply flawed both as methodology and ideology, promising dire consequences for humanity. Today rational individuals poison the atmosphere, deforest the land, deplete the seas, pollute the rivers and conduce life-threatening climatic change, while countless millions die for want of food and water. Always the technological means are elegantly rational to individuals, but they are in pursuit of ends which must ultimately kill us all. The power of rational technology in the modern industrial state means that the problem of reconciling the interests of individuals with those of the community has never been greater.

2 THE ROOTS OF INDIVIDUALISM

The previous chapter spoke of crude forms of liberalism and individualism associated with the Thatcherite rhetoric which found an echo in the hearts of many voters, lending an aura of populist approval attained by few British prime ministers. However, although essentially a product of modernity, an individualism of sorts has a pedigree dating from early times. The ancient Greek Thrasymachus argues in Plato's *Republic* that 'might is right', that the individual has the right to fight to secure self-interest. In Book II of the *Republic*, Glaucon portrays the state not as a community but as a contract between self-interested individuals for mutual safety. There was also the hedonistic philosophy of the Epicureans who believed individual happiness to be the *summum bonum* (chief good) of life. However, for the most part, philosophers regarded egoism as an unnatural and undesirable trait; only in the modern era was it to be elevated as a basis for morality.

Discovering the individual

A crucial philosophical watershed was the Protestant Reformation of the sixteenth century wherein Martin Luther asserted sovereignty of the individual conscience and the right of the individual to commune directly with God, which no human institution, including the Church itself, could overrule. Later, the eighteenth-century Enlightenment advanced the compelling and intoxicating idea that human reason could release for mankind a pattern of unending improvement in science and politics. However, as an overtly political theory individualism comes from Locke out of Hobbes, spawning generations of rational utilitarians including the Philosophical

Radicals and the classical economists. The neo-liberals who gained the Thatcher ear were not midwives to a new intellectual birth. Neither did they advance the tradition of humane liberal thought as developed by thinkers such as Kant, J. S. Mill and Rawls. Rather, they were faith-healers who, with the addition of some vigorous massage and the kiss of life, revived the grey corpses of Locke, Adam Smith, Malthus and others. In this chapter we trace briefly the pattern of individualist thought from the seventeenth century, leading to the grand theory of the market, its proudest manifestation.

The constitutional soil of the seventeenth century was particularly fertile for English political theory. The period shuddered under seismic political activity, with a protracted struggle between King and Parliament, a civil war, a tentative flirtation with republicanism terminated by a restoration of the monarchy and, finally, a constitutional revolution. The downfall of kings and the challenge to the traditional doctrine of a divine right to rule required a new basis for explaining and justifying the allegiance owed to the state. If ever there was a period to inspire thought about the nature of the state, this was it (Skinner 1978: 349), although it was an activity which could seriously endanger the health.

Individualism: the method

We can find the roots of individualism as a method in the approach of Thomas Hobbes (1588–1679), England's greatest political thinker. His self-appointed mission was to harness the emerging scientific spirit of his age, which was dramatically enhancing understanding of the natural world, to the study of society and government. Although captivated by science, he did not see in the experimental and inductive methods of Bacon (for whom he once acted as emanuensis) a paradigm for the study of politics. His object was to apply the 'resolutive-compositive' method of Galileo (to whom he made a pilgrimage to Florence), which entailed deconstructing the subject of study into its constituent elements and reconstructing them in accordance with the laws of logic. The latter operation resembled the method of Euclidian geometry, by which Hobbes was also inspired, deducing complex (perhaps startlingly counter-intuitive) propositions from simple, self-evident axioms.

The axioms

When Hobbes broke down society he came to the individual acting in accordance with certain pyschological principles. These were to be his self-evident axioms, discovered by introspection:

> *Nosce teipsum*, read thy self: . . . whosoever looketh into himself, and considereth what he doth, when he does *think, opine, reason, hope, feare, etc.*, and upon what grounds; he shall thereby read and know, what are the thoughts and passions of all other men, upon like occasion. (Hobbes 1968: 82)

Earnest contemplation of the Hobbesian navel resulted in an exceedingly unflattering portrait of mankind. His most fundamental axiom was that the instinct to avoid death supersedes all others. This was certainly true of Hobbes, whose prudential timidity facilitated remarkable longevity in an age when it was not always politic to voice constitutional views. The law was an iron one: in *De Cive* he argued that every person shuns death 'by a certain impulsion of nature, no less than that whereby a stone moves downward' (Lamprecht 1949: 26). From this could be deduced the idea that all complex willed behaviour was explicable in terms of aversions and appetites, always reflecting the desire for self-preservation. The individual was a calculating machine living a cost–benefit-analysis existence.

Reconstituting society: the state of nature

From these individualist postulates Hobbes deduced a vision of life – a 'state of nature'. This was a nightmare in which egocentric individuals forever torment each other with their selfish ambitions – a war of all against all lived in 'continuall feare, and danger of violent death' (Hobbes 1968: 186). Famously he declared life in nature to be nasty, brutish and short.

Hobbes's state of nature was in all probability a logical abstraction derived from his observation of people in civilized society. 'How, by what advice, men do meet, will be best known by observing those things which they do when they are met' (Lamprecht 1949: 22). He was, in his 91 years, to witness all the constitutional upheavals of the age and saw civil war as a horror from which proceeded 'slaughter, solitude, and the want of all things' (Hobbes 1839: 8). Moreover, and of particular significance, Hobbes's society was becoming a market society where 'it is plain every man regards not his fellow, but his business; if to discharge some office, a certain market friendship is begotten, which hath more of jealousy in it than true love, and whence factions may sometimes arise, but goodwill never' (Lamprecht 1949: 22). Hence the nightmare in nature was not so very far from the reality. He envisaged only one solution to the destructive war of all upon all.

Hobbes's prescription: Leviathan rules

Egoism was not an ethical ideal; it was a cold reality. Hobbes's prescription was that the only way people could be saved from the 'incommodious' life which nature offered was to place themselves voluntarily under an all-powerful, self-perpetuating sovereign (the latter requirement was to avoid war over the succession). Obligation to the ruler was based upon prudence: self-interest was a perfectly sound basis for morality. This was a daring and radical leap in thought, reversing the traditional view that morality could only be derived from nature (conscience) or the will of God, backed by the threat of an eternal netherworld of hell-fire (Macpherson 1962: 76–8). Hobbes believed that he had deduced universal moral obligation from fact; he had determined what *ought* to be from what *was*. This idea was fraught with danger. In placing self-interest before the morality of religion, he relived the fable of Adam. Not only was God cast out, the notion of community with claims above individuals lost meaning; life itself had no purpose beyond individual self-interest.

Paradoxically, although his deductions led to decidedly illiberal conclusions, those who followed his methodology were to find a basis for the liberal state. This could be accomplished by believing that untrammelled egoism in a state of nature was not as bad as Hobbes had imagined. To understand this we must consider a contrasting view of the individual in a state of nature, that of John Locke, the father of classical liberalism.

Individualism: the ethic

Although not dispensing with God, John Locke (1632–1704) placed the individual at the centre of his earthly universe. The idea of the state of nature was again invoked, but unlike those populating Hobbes's jungle, Locke's natural people behaved like English gentlemen. Far from imposing order by means of force, Locke's government required but a minimal role, merely protecting the sacred 'natural rights' bestowed by God.

Individuals in a state of nature possess rights to life, limb and liberty. From these derive a right to the produce of one's own labour, implying a share of the human inheritance of the earth; that is, ownership of property upon which to toil. On the face of it, the right to property is not unlimited. Since no one can have the right to cause another to starve in the midst of God's plenty, the right is restricted to an amount required to sustain life: 'Whatever is beyond this, is more than his share, and belongs to others' (Locke 1988: *Second Treatise*, s. 31). However, Locke's logic led him away from this egalitarian principle.

Locke's prescription

Although not offering a complete institutional model of government, Locke generally wished to see it kept to a minimum. The state must not create rights; it merely protects those already in nature, which should not be removed from people without their consent. Consequently government must be assumed to be based upon a notional contract, implied in the very existence of the society, an assumed 'tacit consent' amongst people to forgo certain natural rights for prudential reasons. Accordingly he supported the idea of limited constitutional government and a separation of powers. This was no absolutist Leviathan with power to appoint its successors, it was the government of a majority. However, Locke's democratic inclinations, like those of other liberals, were limited. Indeed, he is ambiguous, if not two-faced, on the question of the membership of his civil society. When he speaks of the right to life and liberty he includes all, but when he speaks of the right to own goods and estates he reserves them to large landowners. Similarly, when he speaks of a contract into which people enter in order to be ruled, he means all, but when he speaks of a contract for the purpose of ruling he means only those possessing substantial estates. He believed that the poverty of the labouring classes would oblige them to occupy themselves wholly in work, with no time for political mobilization. Indeed, it was the role of the state to prevent this since it 'rarely happens but in the mal-administration of neglected, or mismanaged government'; bad government is not leaving the poor at subsistence level, but allowing them to unite for political action (Macpherson 1962: 224).

The essential meaning of the good life is the freedom to do one's own thing. This entails both the freedom to determine one's ends and the means whereby they may be reached. From this ideal stems the great liberal tradition which was to influence much western constitutional development, supplying the Founding Fathers with a basis for the US Constitution and even influencing the French revolutionaries. In Britain, the pattern of industrial development was to place Locke's individualism particularly close to the constitutional heart.

Deriving the liberal state

From his egalitarian precepts Locke managed the astonishing feat of justifying inequality even to the extent of curtailing the property rights of others, a conclusion most welcome to the large-scale property-owning class, as well as to the newly developing bourgeoisie. It was accomplished through the concept of money. Without money, the production of more food than would be eaten leads to waste and offends God's law. However, money enables excess produce to be sold and the profits stored, eventually to become interest-earning capital. Because Locke found capitalistic appropriation and accumulation in nature, there was no natural restriction on individuals having more than their fair share. He believed this did not contravene the natural right of all to subsistence because those without land have their power to labour, which is also a form of property, carrying a natural right to be alienated for a wage. Indeed, the large landowners, one of whom was Locke himself (Macpherson 1962: 199–208), could not work their land without such an arrangement. The message was also good news for the commercial bourgeoisie to whom labour was life-blood.

Hence Locke's state of nature is no primitive jungle but a fantastical place where one finds not only a natural right to unlimited property, but money, wages and capitalist markets. In effect, Locke says that capitalism is natural and the unequal possession of property a right which people bring to civil society; it is not created by the state and should not be removed by it. This inegalitarian tendency is the paradoxical result of all individualist doctrines; although starting from postulates of equality they reach contrary conclusions. The societies which emerge are not truly atomized but contain competing groups of insiders and outsiders; they are class societies, divided by ownership of property. If this was implicit in Hobbes and Locke it became starkly obvious when individualists invented a world which they believed could work, not by means of government but by clockwork. This delicate, self-regulating mechanism, working with the precision of a Victorian gold-plated pocket-watch, was the market.

The dismal scientists: Leviathan's hidden hand

A new generation of individualists was to accept the atomized, ego-driven vision of society, but rather than postulate a need for an all-powerful sovereign, they were to claim that competitive self-seeking behaviour would itself produce a perfectly agreeable society. The war of all against all would result in harmony, balance and maximum happiness. Hence there was no need for absolutist government and Locke's desideratum of freedom could be the guiding ethical principle. Freedom for the market – the doctrine of *laissez-faire* – meant that the liberal state could turn discord into harmony.

Locke had been acceptable in his time because he had placed a veneer of natural rights over self-interested egoism. By the eighteenth century the possessive, avaricious, individualistic morality was so well accepted that the veneer could be stripped away to lay naked the stark economic utilitarianism beneath. This was to be the project of the classical economists led by Adam Smith, Thomas Malthus and David Ricardo, who earned for the discipline they invented the deserved title 'the dismal science', and of the utilitarians inspired by Jeremy Bentham.

The market: naked as nature intended

The classical economists were essentially utilitarians, arguing that the market, in which each individual acts selfishly, will ultimately make all better off – the great game where the batsman faces the bowler alone but his score augments the team's total with arithmetic certainty.

And God created Adam: the founding father

Adam Smith (1723–90) began a distinguished tradition of Scottish economists which has no doubt contributed to the reputation for the closely guarded sporran of those inhabiting the lands north of the border. He has the greatest claim to the crown of founding father of the discipline. At Oxford he noted with alarm that professors were paid regardless of how much work they did, and consequently did very little. This searing insight was to colour his view of life. The economic system should be designed to align the interest of individuals with diligence, rather than sloth. Self-interest was a far better basis for good behaviour than high moral principle.

Smith travelled to France where he was able to delight in the company of Voltaire, the pre-eminent man of reason, and encountered the physiocrat school of economists, who worked from the underlying premiss that all wealth originated in agriculture where mankind, taking advantage of the hand of God in promoting organic growth, could actually release more wealth than the work put in would normally justify. In 1776 he published his *magnum opus*, *An Inquiry into the Nature and Causes of the Wealth of Nations*, which contained his great thought that the wealth of a nation is the outcome of the efforts of all its members pursuing their own individual self-interest. The general interest is tended, not by any government or individual, but by the ectoplasmic 'hidden hand' for which Smith will ever be remembered.

The market is a wondrous self-regulating mechanism. It would not fall into slump because, as Smith's French disciple Jean Baptiste Say had explained, the quantity produced would always generate the income for its purchase. Aggregate demand would always equal aggregate supply. Left to itself, it would operate for the good of all but, like the delicate clockwork it was, would be irreparably harmed by the intrusion of the clumsy fingers of mankind. Although there were always sceptics, it was not until the Great Depression of the inter-war years that the illusion of all this was to be laid bare.

Smith also laid the theoretical foundation for the factory system, lavishing praise upon the division of labour. His famous example, without which no textbook would be complete, was of a pin factory where ten individuals specializing in minute parts of the operation could manufacture almost 50,000 pins a day, compared with a miserable 20 produced by ten separate individuals (Smith 1976: 8). This was mass production; it could serve mass markets and manufacture mass profits.

Smith coupled this with his theories of trade, arguing for complete freedom across national boundaries, with each country concentrating on commodities for which it was most fitted, in which it had a 'comparative advantage'. Hence he was opposed to the mercantilist state which, with its monopolies and tariffs, was a gilding of the sublime free-market lily. The industrial revolution, increasing the possibilities for factory production and market activity beyond imagination, was to witness Smith's official recognition as a prophet, if not his canonization to the calendar of saints.

David Ricardo and Thomas Malthus: dismal prophets

Smith's mission was taken up by David Ricardo (1772–1823) who, as a stockbroker and Member of Parliament, was supremely fitted to the trade of political economy. Like his friend and fellow economist Thomas Malthus (1776–1834), he believed that the seemingly uncontrollable sexual passion of the masses promised social catastrophe – the population would exceed the power of production. However, once again there were divinely ordained laws to intercede. Population pressure would force down wages so that workers would receive only enough to live on (or even less). In the world of the classical economists, before the full impact of industrialization had been felt, the key figure was the landowner, and the population pressure which reduced wages also increased rents by bringing less fertile land under cultivation. It was a great and elegant law of nature that as the landlords got fatter, so the people grew thinner, ultimately starving and thereby controlling population size with logical elegance.

The case for liberal government became stronger than ever. It was necessary to eschew all measures which might rescue the starving from their fate because this would offend against the natural laws and encourage them to multiply, thereby worsening the problem. State intervention would also be the denial of the economic freedom to pursue self-interest which, as Smith had explained, was crucial for the national good.

The greatest happiness, the greatest profit

However, in truth the market did need the state, a fact recognized by another arch individualist, Jeremy Bentham (1748–1832). Curiously, although fervent in the liberal cause, he rejected the idea of natural rights, describing the reference to 'imprescriptible natural rights' in the French Declaration of the Rights of Man as 'nonsense on stilts'.

Bentham was a philosopher more than an economist, yet his ideas complemented those of the classical free-market thinkers. As befits an individualist, he was profoundly egocentric and, although not a front-rank philosopher, assailed by the most extreme delusions of intellectual grandeur. His individualist proclivities were strengthened by the fact that he found all around him, including his Oxford tutors, extremely stupid. (He omitted to record their feelings about him.) Hermetically ensconced in Queen's Square, with a venerated teapot named Dick, and mice running freely across his barely decipherable manuscripts, he produced reams of pseudo-technical jargon outlining his Felicific Calculus, which was to be nothing less than a master-plan for mankind.

As a utilitarian he drew inspiration from the thinking of David Hume (1711–76) and his entire philosophical system derived from a principle developed by two other utilitarians, Priestley and Hutchinson: 'the greatest happiness for the greatest number'. Eureka! Here was the germ of a principle which could be used to fashion both the law and politics of a nation. Bentham had no patience with conservative and organic theories of the state, nor with the law which venerated the wisdom of the ages; all institutions should be designed on the utility principle.

The conservatism which resisted the constitutional and legal changes he advocated pushed Bentham towards radicalism, a movement completed by acquaintance with James Mill. Together they were the founding fathers of the Philosophical Radical movement which opposed the ancient forces of the landed interests. Bentham placed a profound faith in the idea of legislation as the vehicle for entrenching the utility principle throughout life. He saw the state as a law-making machine and virtually no agency of the nineteenth-century state was left unmarked by his imprimatur.

Although undoubtedly an individualist, Bentham did not entirely share the classical economists' faith in the ability of the hidden hand to produce the maximum happiness throughout society. It was necessary for the law and the state to so design the pattern of rewards and punishments that the pursuit of individual self-interest would conduce the maximum happiness for the greatest number – a conclusion entirely commensurate with the interests of the rising bourgeoisie. Their claim that the market called for a minimal state was entirely bogus; they needed the state and Bentham could be its architect since he shared their basic view of the role of government.

As John Stuart Mill (1806–73), a later utilitarian who was very critical of Bentham's hard and cold logic, explained, Bentham's view of life was of atomistic individuals pursuing their entirely separate pleasures so that the role of the state could be no more than to prevent them from 'jostling one another more than is avoidable' (quoted in Kymlicka 1989: 15). This was the underlying rationale for the state machinery which he so laboriously devised. The complementarity between the ideas of the Philosophical Radicals and the classical economists saw a rigorous institutional revamping to build a state which Lenin was to dub 'the best possible shell' for free-market capitalism.

Bentham's acceptance of the free market and of the dismal laws of the classical economists was demonstrated in the great Poor Law reforms of 1834, pushed through by his acolyte and emanuensis, Edwin Chadwick. These imposed a harshly penal regime of poor relief, with the intention of harmonizing the self-interest of the poor with grindingly hard work. Hence the principle of 'less eligibility' was designed to ensure that conditions in the workhouses were even more appalling than those endured by the meanest-paid person in gainful service of the economy.

The inexorable logic of individualism was leading to a savagely class-based society in which community feeling was replaced by an unrelenting competition – the war of all against all dreaded by Hobbes. The prizes were undreamed-of wealth and power for the winners, but they were the few. Were they bad people? Following their sternly Protestant code they eschewed flagrant voluptuous life-styles in order to accumulate wealth, and their God was as disapproving as they were on the question of sloth. However, the burgeoning of philanthropic societies (which the classical economists condoned, not for aiding the poor, which was bad, but for the elevating effects on the souls of those who gave) suggested that a nagging sense of bourgeois guilt weighed on the minds of some. However, into this world where the poor got poorer and the *nouveaux riches* grew richer at a rate unimagined by the landowners whom they challenged for supremacy, came justification from natural science.

Survival of the richest: free-market Darwinism

In 1859 Charles Darwin (1809–82) published his theory of evolution in the *Origin of the Species*, which accounted not only for origins but also differences in degree. It was in the grand order of things that, as the slugs and snails should inhabit the mud and slime, so the higher primates, with infinitely superior brains, should dominate the high ground of the planet. Darwin's meticulous observations had been conducted amongst life-forms more primitive than those found in the rugged terrain of boardrooms, banks and finance houses, but his thesis, that only the fittest survive, seemed eminently appropriate to a social world based upon competition. It was redolent of the very state of nature envisioned by Hobbes. However, there was no need for the leviathan state since competition was actually good for the soul and for the species. Foremost in this enterprise was Herbert Spencer (1820–1903), who approached his subject of sociology with the pessimism of the practitioners of the dismal science itself.

Members of the bourgeoisie began to understand why they, and not others, found themselves luxuriating at the pinnacle of the great natural pyramid. Spencer was to develop a social version of Darwinism in which the successful and affluent were recognized as the very best of the species. To bourgeois ears this was music of the sweetest kind; rather than grasping parvenus, or sublimely fortunate gamblers, they were the naive heirs of a natural genetic superiority. Indeed, since nineteenth-century Britain dominated the world, they could, without false modesty, lay claim to being the highest life-form yet evolved upon earth. The encouragement of them and their kind represented the vital process of improving the species. By the same token, those living (or dying) in poverty and squalor were the worst, the least fit to survive. Of course, in the eyes of God perhaps no one was entirely useless; their extinction would help strengthen the human race. It was both a civic duty and a scientific responsibility of the rich studiously to avert their eyes from the sufferings and begging bowls of the poor (Spencer 1865: 413).

The prophets triumphant: the wealth of Britain

The ideas of the classical economists were to receive triumphant confirmation in movements of the age. Smith was interested in the wealth of nations and, under his inspiration, that of the British nation grew one-hundredfold. Individualism, self-interest, free trade and comparative advantage were to allow Britain to plunder the world for cheap raw materials, yielding but small profits to their producers, while supplying it with high-profit manufactures. Despite the loss of America, the empire reached its splendid zenith. Britain could reasonably claim to rule, not only the waves, but the continents upon which they washed. The sun never set on this vast territory of hope and glory and, most symbolic of all, no English gentleman abroad could relieve himself without patriotically pondering the legend 'Armitage Shanks' inscribed indelibly in British porcelain.

At home prosperity meant Malthusian population growth and falling wages. In Ireland, where the industrial revolution was held back (following the comparative advantage theory) in order to produce grain to feed English workers, the same population trends saw the rents accruing to absentee English landlords escalate with a joyful buoyancy in the manner ordained by Ricardo. The 1845–7 potato famine was but further reminder of the rigid and dismal rules of the game. Treasury officials kept dutifully out of these economic matters; if the hidden hand decreed that excessive population growth should be curbed by the grim reaper, so be it. It was the hand of God, a stern deity with little affection for the slothful. The repeal of the Corn Laws, a symbolic testimony to accumulating bourgeois hegemony which lowered the price of bread, did not pursue any humanitarian motive; it was to allow cheap grain imports and weaken the position of the old landowners against the new industrial class.

The coming of the liberal state: citizens or beasts?

These triumphant years were to harden the tradition of individualism in British political culture, becoming embedded in a series of constitutional reforms which created the liberal state. The notion of the contract, so central to the process of creating wealth, became the basis for the state itself. The political culture was to portray the state in negative terms as a denial of freedom, only to be tolerated to the extent that it served certain prudential (self-interested) purposes of individuals.

Such an attitude contrasted starkly with the dominant tradition of western thought which originated in the great ancient Greek civilization existing between 800 and 500 BC. This saw the state as much more than a potentially threatening mutual protection agency; it was the very embodiment of the civilized life. A person living outside the state was incomplete – in Aristotle's famous aphorism, 'either a beast or a god'. In seventeenth-century English thought, the individual was lifted from the community; the best life was the one lived outside the state, the best state was the one which kept out of life. The individual appeared to have become a god, or had he been made a beast?

3 TOWARDS THE COMMUNAL STATE: CREATING SOCIAL DEMOCRACY

The nature of the state, a burning issue for thinkers in the seventeenth century, was refocused in Britain during the 1980s with the rise of the New Right which attacked not merely the policies of its political opponents, but the very idea of a social democratic state. What exactly were they attacking? This chapter examines the nature of social democracy, arguing that it alone represents the truly modern state, the highest evolutionary form to have emerged in modern history. Consequently, the attempt to undermine it can only be seen as a retrogressive act.

The evolving state

The feudal state

With the break-up of the Roman empire a new system of labour evolved in Western Europe to replace slavery, based on landlords, 'free tenants' and peasants tied to estates. The social order formed a strict hierarchy from the lord down to the serfs, who were tied to the land within the manorial court but with the right to retain produce for themselves. Labour was not for a wage and production was largely for use rather than exchange. In a balance of mutual obligation, the lord would maintain order and justice through the manorial court. The serf could not be seen in a political relationship with the state, which was restricted to the king and the vassal lords with their independent local centres of power (Poggi 1978: 23). However, the king was not sovereign, being heavily dependent upon the lords for taxes and fighting men (regular consultation with the lords at court provided, in England, the foundations for the Privy Council and Parliament). Additional competition to royal authority came from the towns and the Church. The former emerged from trade, manufacturing and commerce, establishing autonomy through royal charters giving leading citizens the right to administer town life – a source of considerable power. The Church was able to claim supreme authority over the secular rulers on the basis of spirituality, becoming immensely powerful, wealthy and highly bureaucratic.

Under feudalism the organization of the state and the method of production were indissolubly welded. The landowners, like the Roman slave-owners before them, were the rulers; state and economy were one. However, the secular powers challenged the hegemony of the Church in the Reformation of the sixteenth century. Feudalism began to collapse as dues were commutated into rents, military dependence was reduced by the formation of professional armies, and increasingly painful tax burdens were imposed by the centre, disrupting local rule.

The absolutist state
From the collapsing feudal system emerged new states centralized under royal authority, with stronger and more uniform systems of law and more efficient state bureaucracies (Poggi 1978: 60–2). Monarchs were no longer willing to be *primus inter pares* with other nobles, lords and estates. In the sixteenth century Jean Bodin (1530–96) formulated the doctrine of the 'divine right of kings', justifying royal absolutism in terms of the will of God. In Britain, control over the state was made particularly easy owing to the absence of clear racial or religious differences. The Yorkist kings and the Tudors subordinated nobility and Church in the Wars of the Roses and the English Reformation. The state also consolidated its domination over Wales, Ireland and Scotland.

The mercantilist state
The absolutist states were nation-states and their relations with each other became increasingly formalized through diplomatic channels with treaties, alliances and strategic arranged marriages. Trade and commerce widened beyond the local perspective of feudalism so that it became possible to speak of a national economy. A world market emerged based upon colonies, sea power, protected trade routes and the slave trade.

From the mid-sixteenth to the end of the seventeenth century an economic doctrine of mercantilism was predominant. This accorded the state a central role in the economic affairs of the nation. National prosperity and power in international politics were identified with the success of merchants, measured by the accumulation of wealth in the form of gold, the universal currency. The state would impose exchange controls, use naval power to protect the trade routes, impose tariffs, grant monopolies and levy taxes to pay for its activities. It was a state with an explicitly economic role, one which could impinge upon the lives of individuals in the interests of the whole.

A state of nature: the liberal state
It is with the coming of the liberal state that the evolutionary pattern registered a quantum leap. As a product of reason, science and rationality it can be called the modern state, one which broke from the fetters of tradition and convention. The pre-modern states exhibited diverse forms but shared in common a sense of unity or community, manifested in time-honoured patterns of authority and mutual

obligation amongst people. In the liberal state the institutions and law were to be hand made according to the precepts of utilitarianism to bring the egoistical individualistic drives postulated by Hobbes into the ascendant.

At the very heart of the challenge was the irresistible process of industrialization and the rise of capitalism as the predominant way of producing material goods. Traditional communal relationships in the pre-modern states threatened to frustrate the newly emerging commercial practices with their greater efficiency in manufacture, employment and trade. The laws of entail, for example, inhibited the free exchange of property, feudal ties inhibited the mobility and effectiveness of labour and mercantilism inhibited free trade.

In England, the process of change began with the great constitutional eruptions of the seventeenth century as the increasingly powerful commercial classes from the towns allied with a section of the landed gentry to challenge royal authority. The result was the preservation of a 'medieval particularism' inhibiting the sense of a cohesive state. Most of the European nation-states had developed into patriarchal monarchies in which the old disruptive medieval estates were neutered. They became the benevolent monarchies and republics of the early modern period in which governments could be seen as trustees of a collective good beyond individuals (Marquand 1988: 152–5). In Britain, both the Stuarts and Cromwell had, in their different ways, attempted to subjugate particularistic interests but their efforts foundered on the resistance of landowners who retained and controlled their own property.

The eighteenth-century agrarian revolution saw farming increasingly focused on markets rather than for subsistence; wage labour became extensive, land was sold and purchased, and concepts of private property (possessive individualism) were developed. The pressure was to replace the old economy, with its morality of mutual obligation and a just price, with a market economy, in which price was determined by supply and demand and there was no appeal to moral justification beyond the market.

These events were captured on the wing by the new English individualist thought. The idea of the individual, endowed with the natural right to break free from the constraints of tradition and privilege, was in tune with the changing times. The essential value of the new thinking was the freedom of the individual to act without constraint. It offered no moral basis for determining which ends individuals might pursue other than that they were prudentially chosen on the grounds of personal self-interest.

The process was accelerated to a dizzy velocity by the full impetus of the industrial revolution, reaching its splendid zenith by the mid-nineteenth century. In a Herculean age of legislation, often inspired by Benthamism, the bourgeoisie promoted a breathtaking restructuring of the constitutional landscape, leaving virtually no stone unturned. Parliament, the monarchy, the public finance system, the legal system, the civil service, local government, the police force and the army were all radically transformed in the creation of a state fit for capitalism.

Here then was the liberal state with its underpinning liberal political culture in which individualistic values, holding dear Locke's central assumption that property rights are antecedent to society, were fashioned into the great Whiggish tradition. This was the elegant liberal democracy to be detailed by Dicey, its two great pillars the rule of law and parliamentary sovereignty. Yet the liberalism and democracy offered by this state were of a very special kind, leaving people free to trade and manufacture and accumulate vast profits, or free to sell their labour for meagre wages and to die of starvation and cold.

Yet the evidence of economic growth suggested that the essentially fragmentary, individualist liberal state was the one which worked best. As Britain drove on relentlessly to become the richest and most powerful nation the world had ever seen, the bourgeoisie saw little justification for a state power able to subjugate their individual ambitions to some notion of community. They worshipped a stern Protestant God, but when they sang hymns they also remembered Smith, Ricardo, Malthus and Bentham. However, this age of high Victorian confidence did not possess the durability suggested in the granite pillars of the ornate town halls or the sternly utilitarian factories silhouetted against the industrial horizon. The liberal state was to create its own contradictions. Its minimalist precepts could offer no answers to the problem of the alienation of those for whom the legend of freedom meant only the tyranny of the production process, the bosses and the workhouse.

Although James Boswell could delight in the bourgeois virtues of London, for the great mass of ordinary people the new urban way of living contrasted starkly with the one they had been obliged to forsake under the magnetic imperative of the factories. The grey smoking settlements articulated the antithesis of the ideals of communities, providing a festering ecosystem, not only for the bacteria which ravage bodies but for the social germs of crime, prostitution, mistrust, aggression, violence, corruption and loneliness. The dramatic contrasts between poverty and wealth were displayed with provocative braggadocio so that, for the bourgeoisie, made furtive and uneasy by the wealth which should have made them happy, civic duty meant little more than containing the threat of civic unrest. Early philanthropic action as well as the formation of the modern police force pursued this critical objective.

The poverty of liberalism

Despite the paeans sung to the beauties of the liberal constitution and its *laissez-faire* economy, its virtues were not abundantly evident to all. For ordinary people industrialization meant unendurably hard toil, unemployment, sickness and an early grave. German sociologist Ferdinand Tonnies (1855–1936) contrasted modern industrial society with the traditional order through the ideas of *Gemeinschaft* and *Gesellschaft*. The former arose organically through bonds of kinship and affection, but the latter was cold and soulless, a (notional) contract between people for individual mutual advantage, leaving them tense and forever haunted by the spectre of failure and poverty.

Not only did the liberal state leave people with a sense of emotional loss, it failed to deliver its economic promises. Economic slumps and unemployment were not averted by the allegedly self-regulating clockwork of the classical models; the hidden hand appeared arthritic. Moreover, the greatest critic of the liberal state, Karl Marx (1818–83), taunted that the bourgeoisie had created a Frankenstein's monster (the working class) which would turn and overthrow the system. The message appeared all the more horrible to the privileged when contemplated against the backcloth of the French Revolution.

Another figure to inveigh against the classical nostrums entered the world in the year Marx departed it, but the outspoken views of English economist John Maynard Keynes (1883–1946) were studiously ignored. He had not added to his credibility in establishment cicles by publishing *The Economic Consequences of the Peace* (1919), a devastating critique of the victorious allies' determination to extract more in reparations from the defeated Germans than they could afford to pay. Although isolated from public affairs during the inter-war period, he launched a fusillade of biting criticism. Churchill was a particular target; his 1925 decision to return to the gold standard at the pre-war value of the pound was castigated. To injury Keynes added the insult of being right. The repercussions were to reach around the globe, visiting the Great Depression on the US (Galbraith 1977: 209).

Liberalism in the inter-war years was in a state of deep crisis; the doctrines of the classical economists were found wanting as slumps appeared ineradicable and unemployment chronic. As a reaction, two new forms of state emerged which, although starting from opposite ideological poles, were to converge in darkness and repression.

The new absolutists

If modern society was not to be held together by ancient, divinely ordained rules and customs, or by the market, a Hobbesian state of nature began to look like reality. Both communism and fascism sought, albeit in quite different ways, to re-establish a spirit of community, although both collapsed into a form of leviathan state.

The communist state

One of the most dramatic features of the twentieth century was the rise and fall of the communist state, in which civil society and the state were to become one. This Marxian-inspired experiment aimed to supplant the operation of the free market by establishing a command economy. Private property would cease to exist and the state would assume the main functions in civil society, thereby eradicating class rule and exploitation, the natural concomitants of capitalism. Of course the gap between the idea and the reality was a yawning one; real-world communism soon became one of the all-time great political disappointments. The systems established in Russia after the Bolshevik revolution of 1917, in China by the 1940s, and in the eastern bloc after the second world war proved, in their different ways, to be little more than totalitarian regimes. Far from realizing the communal ideal they revered, they were to be characterized by thinkers such as Orwell as the very apotheosis of totalitarianism, dominated by a bureaucratic class showing all the inhumanity of the reviled capitalist bourgeoisie. Like the liberal states they opposed, they denied the essential features of communal life: participation and democracy. Under the legend of 'the dictatorship of the proletariat' came simply dictatorship.

The fascist state

It is impossible to contemplate the modern state without considering fascism, which developed from the 1920s and led the world to the chaos of war. The term was chosen by the Italian Mussolini to designate the movement which carried him to power in 1922. It was intended to embody a communal spirit, its logo a *fasces* – a bundle of rods symbolizing the community beneath an axe-head symbolizing the state's authority. Yet the reality of fascism was characterized by intense nationalism, little democracy, anti-egalitarianism, demagoguery, militarism, racism, anti-liberalism and anti-communism.

Mussolini's fascism accorded the state a central role in the economy through a system of corporatism in which key industrial interests were incorporated into the policy-making process. The economy was organized into workers' syndicates led by politicians, united under corporations resembling medieval guilds which were supposed to mediate between citizens and state – a form of democratic functional representation. However, the effect was to consolidate power under a small elite. Some scholars, such as the communist Gramsci (1891–1937), who was imprisoned by Mussolini, saw this as a necessary development in a capitalist society. In Germany, the harsh economic measures which the allies had obliged Heinrich Brüning to apply left people feeling that Hitler could only be an improvement. Mussolini had hardly given fascism a good name but it was tarnished for ever as it embraced Nazism and other right-wing movements in a disenchanted world which was again to career fatefully into the appalling calamity of world war.

The social democratic state

The liberal model on the one hand, and fascism and communism on the other, suggest a grim future for the modern state, a polarity between Hobbesian anarchy and a chilling leviathan bureaucratic state. However, this was a bogus dilemma, for a middle way was revealed in the idea of the social democratic state.

What is social democracy? Like liberalism, fascism and communism, the term is interpreted widely to refer to both states and political parties. At one time all parties affiliated with the international socialist movement flew the social democratic banner, but the great split between the Bolshevik and Menshevik wings of the Russian Communist Party in 1905 saw the latter commandeer the label as a means of signalling a non-revolutionary, parliamentary approach to social reform, and this sense of moderation remains central. Its broad principles include the following:

1 Capitalism continues as the dominant mode of production and exchange which means that private individuals may own the means of production and the market remains the principal mechanism of allocation.
2 Progressive taxation seeks to modify the inegalitarian effect of capitalism.
3 The state provides a range of investments which will benefit capitalism, such as communications and transport networks, and various concessions and incentives to private industry.
4 The state provides certain important consumption needs such as social services, health care and education on a universal basis.
5 The state takes a prime responsibility for maintaining employment at high levels.
6 Government consults with representatives of both labour and capital on policy-making (pluralism).

Under such a system the state is no longer minimal; its tentacles extend into many areas of civil society, including the economy and the family. However, this is held not to deny freedom but to bestow it; the state is an instrument of social justice.

Hence the social democratic state moderates the effects of capitalism, bestowing equality where capitalism would create gross inequality, maintaining employment where capitalism would demand unemployment and generally harmonizing when disharmony would prevail. Indeed, it can be argued powerfully that modern capitalism cannot survive other than in a social democratic climate. The state absolves employers of the full costs of the labour they consume: their employees are educated and maintained in good health and, when not required, the state will take over the job of supporting them with pensions and income maintenance. In this way it serves to forestall the fatal catastrophe predicted by Marx.

In the social democratic state there must be a consensus; debate between parties is about means rather than ends, about the priorities within a state health or education service, for example, rather than whether or not they should exist. It is important for democracy to be real rather than a charade since any form of class rule must result in policy favouring the dominant elite. Ultimately, the social democratic ideal is seen to produce the closest embodiment of the spirit of community under capitalism by giving people the rights and resources to participate fully in social life.

In contrast to the dismal vision of the classical economists, who saw a scrawny, ill-educated, undernourished, short-lived working population as a necessary condition of capitalism, the Scandinavian countries appeared during the inter-war years as havens of tranquillity, health and prosperity grounded on buoyant economies combining agriculture and industrialization under government orchestration. They had long traditions of constitutional government and 'respectable' labour movements incorporated into the state procedures. Denmark had a coalition social democratic government from the 1920s, while in Sweden the Social Democrats have remained continuously in office since 1932. These maintained well-established systems of social security, generous state health care and education systems and a century-old tradition of public works expenditure. Denmark's economy was largely agricultural while Sweden was more heavily industrialized, demonstrating that social democracy could work in different kinds of economies. In the former, agriculture was based on cooperative principles rather than *laissez-faire*, although this did not prevent the application of technology running ahead of European competitors. Like Keynes, Scandinavian economists believed that public expenditure could create employment, but unlike the Cambridge luminary, their words were not scorned.

The coming of the social democratic state in Britain

Social democratic ideas were circulating in Britain before the post-war era. Indeed, the foundations are often said to have been laid in the social programme of the 1906–11 Liberal government. In 1938 Conservative Harold Macmillan had resoundingly declared:

> It is both possible and desirable to find a solution of our economic difficulties in a mixed system which combines state ownership, regulation or control of

certain aspects of economic activity with the drive and initiative of private enterprise. (Macmillan 1938: 185)

Yet the British social democratic state was essentially a post-war creation, arising phoenix-like from the ashes of war. In the first world war ordinary people had been urged to fight and die for a *status quo ante* of capitalism, privilege and aristocracy promising little in the way of equality. Those who volunteered often did so in the expectation that conditions at the front would be better than those in the satanic mills, factories and mines at home. The depression and class conflict of the inter-war years confirmed that people had indeed fought for king and country and for little else. Popular enthusiasm for a second enterprise required more tangible benefits.

Promises, promises

Hence it is not surprising that the second world war saw considerable social planning and fervent promises from the establishment of better days ahead. The presence of Labour politicians in the coalition greatly enhanced the credibility of the agenda. The most extravagent promise was contained in the Beveridge Report (1942), seen as the blueprint for a new welfare state and, coupled with this, a white paper on a national health service. In addition, Beveridge chaired the less-known committee which produced the report *Full Employment in a Free Society* (1944). The following year he expanded his view of state-maintained full employment:

> The main instrument of a full employment policy is . . . a new type of budget based on man-power. With this must go many subsidiary measures . . . to guide the location of industry . . . to guide the free movement of labour from job to job and from area to area; to set up collective outlay guaranteeing a market and price in meeting essential needs; to regulate and steady the process of private investment; to extend the public sector of industry, wherever extension is needed. (Beveridge 1945: 63)

Although the political class had been made increasingly uneasy with the liberal tradition and *laissez-faire* since the late nineteenth century, the doubt was now official. The new social democracy was to be a gospel according to Keynes.

The coming of Keynes

Social democracy's commitment to capitalism made Keynes's doctrines of incalculable importance. Although a knight in shining armour of sorts, Keynes came not to slay the dragon but to incarcerate it for its own protection. In his *magnum opus, The General Theory of Employment, Interest and Money* (1936), he rejected the orthodox belief that the free market would automatically find an equilibrium (where aggregate demand equalled aggregate supply) at the point of full employment. Classical economists had argued that savings would always be invested; a rise in saving would produce a fall in interest rates, raising investment until the two were equal and the economy operated at full capacity with no shortage of aggregate demand and no unemployment. Keynes argued that an equilibrium could exist at a point below the full capacity of the economy as a result of a tendency of firms and individuals to save more during a recession (when aggregate demand is falling). Investment would not seem worth the risk to self-interested wealth-holders.

Moreover, cuts in wages designed to increase employment would only deepen the recession by lowering aggregate demand still further.

To counter this the state should step in to break the cycle by stimulating demand through public works (building schools and roads, for example). This would trigger a multiplier effect throughout the economy. Public expenditure would be financed not by taxation (which would counteract the intended increase in aggregate demand) but by borrowing, utilizing the unused savings. Such a policy implied abandoning the hallowed liberal principle of the balanced budget in favour of the shocking idea of a deficit.

Although the endemic depressions of the inter-war years gave little support to the old orthodoxies, it took nothing less than full-scale world war to force Keynes's arguments through obdurate establishment skulls. Expenditure on waging war (far exceeding what would have been required in peacetime) triumphantly confirmed his thesis by miraculously eliminating unemployment.

The long boom

The official capitalist seal of approval was placed on the Keynesian solution in the Bretton Woods agreement of 1944. Here 44 nations assembled to mastermind the post-war economic recovery of the capitalist world and avoid the mistakes of the vengeful and myopic 1919 Treaty of Versailles. Under Keynes's dominant presence the conference established an international system for a capitalist world economy. Although he died in 1946, the agreement heralded an era to bear his name. During this era the western economies grew (most of them more rapidly than the British). Governments seemed able to iron out slumps, unemployment remained low while output soared and prices were held stable. The period was to be labelled a 'long boom' in which capitalism under government management really seemed to work. It was thought to be a future of undiminishing abundance, providing a sound bedrock for comprehensive welfare programmes. Whether a direct result of Keynesian techniques, or the working out of a greater economic 'Kondratieff cycle', capitalism gained a human face, making it part of the reality of social democracy.

The great consensus

Although Churchill did not support the Beveridge proposals, and the medical profession reneged on the health service promises, the momentum was not to be resisted and the 1945 Labour landslide demonstrated that people were not prepared to take the wartime promises lightly. Indeed, the most significant point about the social democratic era was not that Labour gained control of government, but that the Conservatives in opposition accepted the new order. This signalled the emergence of a great post-war consensus to be characterized as 'Butskellism' in an etymological coupling of Gaitskell, Labour's leader, and Butler, architect of the Conservatives' new social democratic realism. It was more than a coupling, for some (Vaizey 1983) it looked more like a *ménage à cinq*, an uneasy bedfull in which Conservatives Macleod and Boyle embraced Labour's Gaitskell and Crosland, all under the voyeuristic eye of Richard Titmuss who, from the urban cloisters of the London School of Economics, fashioned a new academic discipline to stand alongside that of economics: Social Administration. The old discipline studied the allocation of resources according to the iron laws of supply and demand, the new one was concerned with allocation according not to what people could afford, but what they needed. Indeed, it was more than this. Social democracy caught the spirit of the age; civil servants, journalists and academics breathed the new *Zeitgeist*. Emerging from the self-effacing shadows of liberalism the state became fashionable and stylish.

A *modern state*

The definition of the modern state is arguable. Weber saw it in terms of size and rationality, characterized as 'a professional administration, specialized officialdom, and law based on the concept of citizenship' (Weber 1961: 233). T. H. Marshall developed the citizenship theme, ascribing to it three rights components: civil, entailing the freedom for the market economy and capitalism; political, facilitating democracy; and social, enabling people to participate fully in social life (Marshall 1950: 10–14). These had been united in earlier stages of the evolution of the state but were driven asunder by liberalism, with its sharp division between civil society and the state. The social democratic state recombines them, thereby rekindling a spirit of communal life. In this sense it is the true modern state.

Yet the British social democratic state was not to be without blemishes. Starcrossed with high-vaulting ambition and a legacy of individualism deeply etched into the culture, it was to meet its *pons asinorum* in the 1970s. There were more enemies lurking in dark recesses than were apparent during the days of its pomp, and when it looked vulnerable they, as the New Right, were not slow to produce the daggers beneath their robes.

4 THE SINS OF THE FATHERS: DID SOCIAL DEMOCRACY FAIL?

Ambition: an age of reason

The dawn of social democracy seemed to offer unparalleled scope for the application of reason to society's problems. The most resonant paean to this brave new world was intoned by Anthony Crosland in *The Future of Socialism* (1956). In this view, the state possessed a limitless capacity to make things happen. A new political climate, coupled with technical and statistical developments, meant that it was no longer the ectoplasmic hidden hand on the tiller of the economy. The state possessed the power and ability to determine key variables such as the division of total output between consumption, investment, exports and social expenditure and to regulate economic growth.

Although capitalism remained, it was reformed almost beyond recognition. Modern businesses were now owned by a disparate group of impersonal share-holders, all decisions being made by a new class of professional managers bearing little resemblance to the exploitive owner-managers of the nineteenth century. This state was no committee for managing the affairs of the bourgeoisie (see p. 97); those with hands on the levers of power were 'certainly not the pristine class of capitalists' (Crosland 1956: 29).

A foundation stone of this great edifice of optimism was financial. There would be no political problem in paying for social democracy since state-driven economic growth would ensure an ever enlarging cake so that the rich (of whom Crosland was one) would pay more in taxes without actually feeling poorer themselves. All would take place within a spirit of consensus extending across a wide range of social and economic matters. Crosland was clearly impatient with what he saw as outmoded and relentless class-based sloganizing from the Labour left. In the new society all state policies would require the approval of the unions, gained through reasoned consultation; there was no place for talk of overthrowing capitalism. In this atmosphere one could speak meaningfully of a communal state, one which guaranteed the quality of life of all members. Like Macbeth's, Crosland's ambition was high vaulting; was it doomed, like that of the ill-fated thane of Cawdor, to o'erleap itself?

Ambition which o'erleaps itself

As the new era unfolded it became evident that the vision was based upon a number of false hopes. The underlying idea that the power of reason would reach every corner of society was naive, as was the corollary that state and economy could be manipulated like Plasticine. The brave new world could not so easily break free from the fetters of the old. In a culture which venerated constitutional continuity, the architecture of the nineteenth-century master-planners, who had shaped the pillars and stanchions of the state in accordance with the liberal tradition, was allowed to remain. The ancestral voices would not be silenced; the sins of the fathers would be visited upon the sons through the state machinery, the political culture and the economy.

Anatomy of the social democratic state

Although the era was to be one of reform, there remained a fidelity to the hallowed British tradition of constitutional conservatism; the old institutional structure was to be preserved largely unmolested. This was legitimated variously but the justification lay mainly in the liberal doctrine of the neutral state, the sleek Rolls-Royce, ready to veer left or right at the touch of the power-assisted steering wheel. There was also the culture of the Labour Party, with its deferential commitment to parliamentary socialism. Its solicitous attention to the sensitivities of an establishment already shell-shocked by the Labour landslide cautioned against ramming home the advantage with a thoroughgoing constitutional rethink.

Yet grafting new onto old is dangerous constitutional horticulture. This had been recognized by the Fabian-dominated Haldane Committee on the Machinery of Government in 1918, which had faced a similar though less dramatic task of post-war social reconstruction. To prevent the cot death of the infant welfare state the committee had insisted that services be placed in the hands of specially created departments rather than entrusted to the tender mercies of the penny-pinching Treasury and the harshly penal Home Office. The same institutional prudence did not prevail in 1945.

In the giant's kitchen

The grandeur of the ancient organs of state was to render the new ministers like overawed figures in the pantomime giant's kitchen and their political courage could not match their ambition. Hence the social democratic state was not seen to require a new constitution. It would remain 'unwritten', with no bill of rights; people would remain unwilling subjects with liberties (held to be bestowed in nature) won from a potentially evil state, not bestowed by a benevolent one. The electoral system would continue on the distorting first-past-the-post principle which had served to keep Labour out of Parliament in the first place, and a fully-fledged aristocracy, the House of Lords, and public schools would stand in the midst of the social democratic state as mocking reminders of a two-nation culture.

The epicentre of the new state machine was the august Whitehall complex where the very corridors spoke of ancient power. Beyond this was a centralist Benthamite municipal structure and a quasi-independent sector placed out of range of the eyes and ears of democracy, including a newly minted National Health Service, a range of *ad hoc* institutions and a collection of state-owned industries.

Mandarin culture

The nineteenth-century model of the civil service had been designed by Messrs Northcote and Trevelyan, whose momentous 1854 report sought to replace old elitism with new under the guise of meritocracy. The measure of merit was proficiency in the classics, pre-eminently the preserve of the scions of the bourgeoisie, finely finished on the smooth public school–Oxbridge honing stone. Hence, from the first, the recruitment procedure was in reality an exclusion ritual, an instrument of bourgeois class hegemony. The pattern showed remarkable durability and was even able to withstand the withering criticisms of the Fulton Committee (1968), which castigated the 'cult of the amateur' and poured scorn over spurious arguments about the superiority of generalists over specialists.

Hence the custodians of social democracy were from the same social stratum as those heading industry, commerce, the City, the army, the Church and so on. They were to run an education system to which they would not entrust their offspring, a welfare state they would never need, and hospitals in which they would never queue. Any bureaucratic commitment to social democracy could come only through chance encounters of the sons of privilege with radical dons and secret societies in the commodious environs of Oxbridge, in a climate more of treason than reason, with more affinity to the world of Le Carré than Beveridge (Boyle 1979). All was lovingly preserved and no attempt made to widen the social basis of recruitment. Labour leader Attlee was to speak sycophantically of the legendary political impartiality of the silken-tongued mandarins.

Family silver

The famous clause 4 of the Labour Party constitution had established public ownership of the means of production, distribution and exchange as a central plank in the party platform. However, it was decisively jettisoned by the revisionists. The economy was to be a mixed one and the public enterprises were to operate competitively, under the control of members of the old capitalist class sitting as board members. It was made a pious constitutional principle that they should be at 'arm's length' from Parliament. Far from being the model employer hoped by some, the state preserved the appalling tradition of labour relations which it inherited from the archetypal capitalists of old. Economically, the problem of running the industries commercially but with sensitivity to the national interest was never resolved; boards, government and Parliament coexisted in a state of continuing tension.

Crossing the state portals

Under the control of elected representatives of communities, local government was to be a vital link in the new state. Nineteenth-century council chambers were no havens of local democracy, being dominated by local capitalist bigwigs, and under a Benthamite spirit of centralism Whitehall saw the municipalities as outposts for implementing national policy. With the rise of the Labour Party, however, they became the site of vigorous political action, sometimes radical as in Poplarism, though more characteristically inspired by Fabian gradualism. This offered the new social democracy an unrivalled means whereby ordinary folk might set foot over the sacred portals of the state in the spirit of community and democracy.

Yet the 1945 Labour government chose to place its faith almost exclusively in the central institutions; its landslide victory offered the taste of the red meat of Westminster, creating little appetite for the thin gruel of municipalization. Although local authorities were to be given a key role in the welfare state, this was confined to obedient stewardship, justified on the grounds that local discretion would produce variations in standards – anathema to a party committed to the ideal of equality. The result was the rise to pre-eminence of a breed of municipal technocrats, those with the professional skills to put policy into practice. Local government became a seed-bed for two of the most adventitious weeds of social democracy, technocratic elitism and paternalism, both threatening to erode the dignity of citizens (Pahl 1975: 207). In addition, there were racist and sexist dimensions to the problem. Notwithstanding the fact that most welfare state clients were women, the poor, and the ethnic minorities, local bureaucracies became bastions of white maleness making assumptions of 'compulsory altruism' and a female caring role was built into the logic of social administration (Land and Rose 1985).

The nation's health

The National Health Service (NHS) was at once the flagship of the new society and one of its most compromised ideals. The idea that health should be an equal right of all, regardless of wallet size, was deeply symbolic of the communal principal. The wartime white paper had promised a comprehensive service under democratic control. However, the cessation of hostilities in Europe was counterpointed by some vicious fighting on the home front, a starkly visible crack in the much-vaunted consensus which had sustained Britain through the long dark nights of wartime blackout. The medical interests became more solicitous of their professional health than that of the nation (Klein 1989), and in place of democracy they installed a psuedo-local-government system with specially created health authorities under the control of non-elected, medically dominated boards.

This professional dominance secured official acceptance of a medical rather than a social model of health, ensuring that hi-tech, curative medicine, technologically exciting and more remunerative, was the order of the day. A collectivist approach entailing community medicine, health education, anti-pollution policies and preventive measures was to be relegated to a back seat. Moreover, in the supposed egalitarian haven of comprehensive health care for all there remained a malignant class factor: inequalities in wealth were replicated in health. The middle classes were less often ill, their offspring negotiated the cervix with greater success and, having done so, enjoyed a longer sojourn between womb and tomb (Black 1980).

Seeking social justice

At the very heart of the social democratic vision lies the idea of social justice. The untrammelled market is seen to promote unfairness which must be mitigated by the state. The Beveridge Report (1942) declared that the negative rights venerated by liberals were to be augmented with rights positively conferred by the state: to health, education, housing, income and employment. Market weakness (poverty) was not to prevent people availing themselves of certain important goods and services. This meant that the state was to be an egalitarian force, taking from the haves in order to assist the have-nots. Or was it?

Pussy-footing equality

In the best Fabian traditions there was to be no socially disruptive attack on the pattern of wealth or earning; Beveridge was no Robin Hood and would not give the rich uneasy nights. His monumental system of income support aimed not to redistribute income from rich to poor, but from one point in an individual's life cycle to another, a flat-rate system of insurance inherited from Lloyd George's 1911 legislation. Regressive not progressive and, in the style of cold Victorian philanthropy, it aimed to make people stand on their own feet. Such measures could be expected to keep the rich happy by preserving the pattern of prestige and snobbery at a symbolic level while removing the real effects of inequality in key areas of life. It was the kind of approach which Tawney (1931) had termed a 'strategy of equality', although it could never be expected to do more than promote an equalizing tendency.

In the event it did less than this: inequality actually increased as the better-off proved far more adept at availing themselves of welfare state largesse (Townsend 1979; Halsey et al. 1980; Le Grand 1982). For some critics the strategy may be said to have failed because it was one of pussy-footing. If equality was to be a goal of social democracy then a more radical attack would be required, addressing the root causes of inequality – disparities in income and a veritable Everest of inherited wealth. Le Grand declared that the reformers dwelt in a Cloud-cuckoo-land and he labelled them 'The Dreamers' (Le Grand 1982: Ch. 2).

The hidden feather bed

No only did the better-off show themselves more adept at using the overt welfare state, a hidden welfare state emerged to shower them with a glittering array of benefits, including tax relief on mortgages and private pension schemes, investment incentives, charity status for private schools, student grants, miscellaneous tax breaks and so on (Field 1982). The cost of this bounty was twice that of formal state benefits and it was tax on ordinary people's incomes which provided the funds.

Hence the welfare state was stunted at birth. Marxists could find ample evidence that the new state was as much an instrument of capitalism as ever. The new academic discipline of Social Administration (see p. 26) began to detail its working and evaluate its effectiveness. Many of the findings of the new breed of scholars such as Townsend and Abel Smith were critical. Yet others seemed content enough; indeed, there was no real attack from the discipline of Public Administration, where the tradition of scholarship remained largely of a liberal apologist genre, at pains to extol the sublime elegance of the British civil service and the subtleties of conventions like ministerial responsibility. Many of the scholars were ex-members, their critical faculties neutered. Sir John Hoskyns, brought in by Margaret Thatcher to investigate this closed world, noted an ethos in which:

> No one is qualified to criticise . . . unless he has first hand experience of working in it. But if he has worked in it, then there is a convention that he should never speak about it thereafter except in terms of respectful admiration. (Hoskyns 1984: 3)

The common sense of individualism

Institutions cannot in themselves create a state. They must have spiritual as well as physical foundations embedded in a culture of attitudes and assumptions to support and confer legitimacy. The cultural foundations of British social democracy were to prove liable to subsidence.

Initially the Labour landslide suggested a cultural sea change; the people had had enough of rule by their betters. The forces of capitalism were thrown into turmoil. Alarmed Conservative leader Winston Churchill embarked upon a tour of the US to seek solace and the Americans, for their part, contemplated cutting off aid to stem the feared rise of communism. Yet although Labour's star soared to its apogee in the social democratic era, the party actually ruled for only 12 of the 29 years between 1945 and 1974. Moreover, the New Right was easily able to mount an annihilating attack on the New Jerusalem of the welfare state; indeed, its walls were more like those of crumbling Jericho. Why was this?

The answer takes us back to the individualist tradition permeating Britain's constitutional history. The promise of social democracy to preserve a system of capitalism with a lineage stretching back to the eighteenth century meant that, from the first, it was cursed to nurture the seeds of its destruction.

Celebrating the individual

British political culture developed a particularly weak notion of the state and its powers. The seventeenth-century victory over the Stuarts by the landed interests allied with the rising bourgeoisie had made a virtue of the limitation of state authority and devalued the sense of nation as community. Yet individualism favours a narrow class interest rather than the community as a whole. Why should such an ideology suffuse an entire culture? The answer lies in the politics of the mind. Our thoughts are not as free as we think.

Antonio Gramsci believed that in a capitalist society the bourgeoisie could always exercise hegemony over the mass through a unique ability to influence minds. This enabled him to explain why western capitalism moved no nearer the political collapse forecast by Marx. The capitalist class is able to shape the dominant ideology by controlling key institutions such as schools, churches, the public bureaucracy, the professions and the mass media, constructing a popular view, or prevailing 'common sense', of the way things must be.

This dimension of politics was also recognized by the Marxist Frankfurt School in the 1920s and 1930s, a leading member of which was Herbert Marcuse (1898–1979), who left Germany for the US when the Nazis came to power. In his influential work, *One Dimensional Man* (1964), he depicted the mass within a capitalist society as entirely submerged, with no potential for resistance or change. Bourgeois states manipulated mass consciousness, so circumscribing free action that, despite seemingly liberal constitutions, they were essentially totalitarian. Ironically, the technology supposed to liberate and rationalize was a potent agent of enslavement, enhancing material prosperity to the extent that ideas of revolution seemed absurd, and strengthening the claims of the dominant class that their ways, powers and privileges were right and proper.

Hence there developed in British political culture a subtlety which made possible a comprehensive panoply of democratic rights while ensuring that democracy itself remained limited. This was the intention behind the great nineteenth-century constitutional reforms masterminded by the bourgeoisie. According to great chronicler Walter Bagehot (1963), the constitution was to be something which the mass could admire and gawp at – a stately home with clear 'keep out' signs erected at all its portals. Like the Long Room at Lord's, or the lawns of Balliol, the state was for the few.

Although elections are free, Parliament and local government are emasculated; although the press is not actually owned by the Conservative Party, it is right wing in orientation because of the pattern of ownership by media barons with mammoth empires; although the state administration is a meritocracy, it is socially elitist; although the BBC remains formally at an arm's length, it is harassed by government. Yet the British were generally content with all this; the political culture was found to be a deferential one where ordinary people were confident that a political elite could be trusted with the job of shaping their lives (Almond and Verba 1963). At the heart of the complex panoply of justification or legitimation lay the ideology of individualism capable, like Mephistopheles, of assuming many guises and appearing in many places. Here lay the explanation for the fact that in an industrialized country with a huge working class purporting to be a social democracy, the Conservatives have been the natural party of government.

The anti-state society

The individualist society is necessarily the anti-state society. In Britain nobody loves a bureaucrat. Ordinary folk need not peruse the recondite works of Weber or share the nightmares of Orwell, Kafka and Koestler to dread the *Darkness at Noon*. Civil servants, and their tea-drinking penchant, are unloved if not loathed, the local government official ranks even lower, and the army of social workers, community health workers and so on must endure perpetual denigration as busybodies, snoopers and do-gooders. Before the 1980s teachers and nurses may have been exempt from a general tarring with the anti-statist brush, but considerable efforts were made to confirm in the public mind their scurrilous and unprofessional nature and, in the case of the first category, their long, idle holidays. Recourse by these groups to industrial action in support of legitimate claims was portrayed by the right as a dereliction of professional duty, an uncaring contempt for children and patients.

However, there is one category of public servant which the machinery of hegemony seeks to protect. With visits to the schools, cycling proficiency courses, friendly community officers and an unending diet of exciting TV dramas, great efforts are made to assure citizens that the police forces of Britain are not racist, sexist, violent or given to the extraction of false confessions. The common sense must be that strong forces of law and order are the bedrock of civilization as we know it. At the same time, the individualist culture gives to its police force the dirty job of containing the tensions it creates.

As cold as charity

The nineteenth-century view of social assistance was coloured by the idea of charity. Although good for the soul of the giver, it was bad for the receivers, who would lose the will to fend for themselves. Popular consciousness did not expunge this taint in the post-war era. Recipients of services were not citizens with rights, but scroungers. The right-wing Institute of Economic Affairs argues that the provision of welfare services in Britain is against popular wishes, including those of recipients (Hall 1979: 18), while New Right thinkers even suggest that a reduction in welfare provision is doing a favour to those who lose its benefit (Harris and Seldon 1979).

Taxing times

Nowhere is the bending of the mass mind greater than in the sphere of taxation. The popular vocabulary is bejewelled with anti-tax expletives: 'the tax burden', 'crippling taxes', even 'bloody taxes'. Taxation is said to stifle initiative and undermine the economy. This is not surprising, for a society that does not like the state will not want to pay for it. Opposition can be traced back to Locke himself, who regarded it as an absurdity that the state, designed to protect the right to property, could steal it, although he was forced to accept the paradox that the protection of wealth cost money (Macpherson 1962: 254).

With deep symbolism, Margaret Thatcher devoted her short-lived legal career to tax cases, and income tax cuts were one of the few hard promises made in her first party manifesto. In fact, in four years as leader of the opposition, proselytizing with unquenchable zeal, she never made a speech without a ritual lament. 'We all need incentives', she would proclaim, and the Olympian top rates were punitive 'symbols of envy' (Young 1990: 146).

In this culture, tax avoidance contains the stuff of nobility, and the chastening thought that 'there is no such a thing as a free lunch' is confounded through the concept of the tax-deductible business repast. Moreover, mortgage repayments, insurance schemes and so on can often be counted against tax, producing a veritable welfare state of greater generosity than anything dreamed of by the most fervent socialist (see p. 32). Even tax evaders, particularly if they are celebrities, gain visible media and public support. In such a society the welfare state is portrayed not as an asset, but as a burden on enterprise and initiative. A major part of the New Right diagnosis of the failures of the British economy was that its costs had 'crowded out' other, more productive, forms of investment.

The joking society: 'Take my mother-in-law – please!'

It is said that we all like a laugh and there are a number of stock funny subjects in any culture. Many of ours are anti-social-democratic ('This bloke walks into the social security office'), anti-liberal ('Have you heard the one about the two queer vicars?'), sexist ('There was this blonde – big girl!') and racist ('There was a Paki, an Irishman and a Russian'). In similar vein, nationalized industries, trade unionists, local councillors and state bureaucrats are variously satirized or mocked. It is not only comedians who make the jokes; the press contribute to the hilarity, inventing amongst other things the zany 'loony left', a lively farce that was to run throughout the 1980s. Yet popular humour is no laughing matter; it is part of the establishment game to deride those who would upset the constitutional applecart – a far more effective means of control than bringing out the Special Patrol Group. There are of course 'alternative' comedians such as Ben Elton, but they remain within certain constraints of political propriety, their outrageousness more usually confined to saucy sexual matters. The very appellation 'alternative' demonstrates that they are the exception with proves the rule.

Whether or not the jokes are good, they are important agents of socialization, creating the terms of the basic common sense of social life that all reasonable people will endorse, a common sense in which the left is loony, scroungers are lazy, the poor are careless, and the rich are rich because they work hardest. We all laugh, but perhaps the joke is on us.

The exclusive society

Locke's democratic theories presupposed a society from which the majority were excluded, a restriction approved by the bourgeoisie when they demanded the franchise extensions in the nineteenth century. The trick was to ensure the Lockean limitation within the outward framework of democracy. Although complex it was largely accomplished, Britain becoming a nominal democracy while retaining elitism in education, the army, the Church, the state administration, the judiciary, business and industry and so on.

Venerable London clubs allow the select to greet and meet in seclusion, while in the masonic world the symbol of community, the handshake, became another exclusion rite. The sporting calendar is dominated by ritualistic events at which ordinary people are not made particularly welcome – Cowes, Royal Ascot, the Lord's test, Wimbledon and the like. In all these there are sacred 'no go' zones – the Royal Box, the Royal Enclosure, the Long Room at Lord's and so on. The culture of exclusion is topped by an ancient but very much alive aristocracy, on public display in certain country houses and in the House of Lords, where they exercise a divine right to rule which the males of the species have long believed their birthright.

The effect extends to cultural and social life, pompous occasions at the Albert Hall and Covent Garden being largely festivals for the upper classes. Classical music and drama, which often contain a subversive message like, say, *The Marriage of*

Figaro or Beethoven's *Fidelio*, not to mention a wealth of literature from Dickens to Tolstoy, is also held to be the preserve of the elite, while the masses are fed the pap of pop. Performers like Nigel Kennedy and Luciano Pavarotti are generally frowned upon for cultivating a populist appeal.

The exclusion processes are of immense political importance and various means have been employed to forestall the 'tyranny of the majority'. Disraeli's notion of one-nation Conservatism was crucial in this; rather than form a political party of its own, the working class was to be wedded to the old elite and vote accordingly. Of course, the symbiosis which brought rich and poor together envisaged one in the castle and the other remaining with feet planted very firmly in the mud at the gate. The lower orders were to support the Conservatives in the polls but were not expected at their hunt balls or garden parties.

The fragmented society
Individualism does not favour communal feelings within the state and the hegemonic forces will promote fragmentation. Britain, throughout its social democratic era, remained beneath the façade a class-divided society; with its north–south chasm and the running sore of Northern Ireland, it was a disunited kingdom.

The class system is preserved as carefully as were the Hanging Gardens of Babylon and is scarcely less a wonder of the world. One of the key factors in its survival is the claim that it does not exist. What people see is merely a whiff of smoke, an ectoplasmic echo from a bygone age; Britain is said to be a classless society. Yet the contrasts between the inner-city slums and the leafy glades of Metroland seen from the railway carriages speeding from the desolate north to link with Network South East are no chimera; Britain remains replete with the symbols of its two-nationhood.

In addition, indelibly sexist and patriarchal at all class levels, British culture contains a hidden gender. The end of the war saw the men returning to drive women from the workplace on the grounds of their domestic responsibilities. Individualist thinking has a special version of the family unit: the individual plus dependents. This family requires a particular role for the female of the species: caring for the male and rearing the children. Social democracy reinforced this through largely illegitimate assumptions about the woman's role as a complementary, though unpaid, part of the welfare state (Land and Rose 1985). The working class, with fewer career opportunities for women, is probably more sexist than any other, while the tabloid press and women's magazines reinforce the homemaker image.

In addition, the experience of empire gave to British culture a lingering aftertaste of master-racism. Paradoxically, this increased during the social democratic era as a result of immigration, which the mother country encouraged as a source of cheap labour (Walvin 1984). The slogan 'If you want a nigger for a neighbour, vote Labour' won a dramatic victory for a Conservative candidate in Smethwick, and although he was labelled a 'parliamentary leper', the Labour Party quickly tightened its policy on immigration. Enoch Powell's incendiary speeches roused London dockers to clamorous adulation, probably helping to propel the Conservatives into office in 1970. A Gallup poll revealed an alarming 75 per cent of the population sympathetic to his position (Marwick 1982).

The culpable society
Like Marx, Locke observed the opiate qualities of Christian discipline: 'The view of heaven and hell will cast a slight upon the short pleasures and pains of this present state' (Macpherson 1962: 225). However, the classical economists discovered in the market a divinely ordained system of rewards and punishments operative in this world as well. In the reasoning of the individualists, everything we are is the result of our own efforts; we are to blame for our misfortunes and have no right to envy the material success of others. Culpability can also explain inequality. In the great meritocratic ladder of education and life the rewards are believed to go to the deserving rather than the lucky. Right-wing politicians blame inner-city violence by unemployed youths on their innate propensity towards evil. The culpability thinking was exemplified in the 1980s by James Anderton, Chief Constable of Greater Manchester, when he declared that drug addicts and AIDS sufferers 'dwelt in a cesspit of their own making'. Women can be particularly indicted in the culpable society, available as scapegoats for a variety of social pathologies including juvenile crime, poor educational standards, illegitimate birth, child abuse, and even rape. The notion of personal culpability was to lie at the emotional heart of the attack on the welfare state. Why should the hardworking be expected to support the indolent and slothful?

Steering the economy: the undevelopmental state

British political culture accommodated some parts of the social democratic package more readily than others. From the Liberal programme of 1906–14 to the post-war Beveridge welfare state there was always a greater willingness to protect losers from the ravages of the market than actually to dare to interfere with the decisions of businessmen acting according to their own perceptions of self-interest (Marquand 1988: 150). Yet the post-war vision of social democracy saw the welfare state umbilically attached to the body of the economy, feeding upon the life-blood of growth. It was not enough to avert unemployment, the economy should boom.

Decline and fall
In fact the economy did boom, after a fashion, but only as part of the long boom of western capitalism – the post-war recovery in world trade promoted by the Bretton Woods agreement and a new technological revolution. Harold Macmillan captured the boom spirit in his famous one-liner: 'Most of our people have never had it so good'. Yet the hard truth was that, in these years of plenty, the British economy was languishing in relative decline. Rivals were having it even better, evoking the suspicion that Shakespeare's island demi-paradise was one populated by fools.

By the 1960s discussing decline was one of Britain's few growth industries. Although journalists, academics and politicians vied with each other in diagnoses and prescription, there was broad agreement that growth was too slow and investment was lacking in the new high-tech, high-profit industries. The explanation for the failure can again be found in the sins of the fathers. In the first place there were the state agencies, preserved in the individualist aspic of the nineteenth century, unable fully to understand their new positive role. More important was the culture of individualism, at its most virulent in industry, the spiritual home of capitalism.

In the kingdom of the blind

Nothing amongst the constitutional Victoriana stood out more ostentatiously than the agency placed at the very heart of the process: HM Treasury. Reared under the austere Gladstone, he of the balanced budget, the department was never able to come to terms with its new role (Hutton 1986). Although *laissez-faire* had been officially renounced, there remained in the bureaucratic mind a dread of initiative, of making choices (Shonfield 1965: 93). While *dirigiste* traditions made the exercise of discretion second nature to the French official, to the mandarins of Whitehall it was a hazardous foray into a alien world, to be avoided as much as the Clapham omnibus. Demand management was interpreted as a languid passivity: exuding an aura of coy femininity unwilling to initiate the embrace, the disdainful mandarins were indeed the very 'apotheosis of the dilettante' (Balogh 1968). Moreover, the fact that the blind were prepared only to be led gave little hope if it was the blind who were to lead. Cairncross (1985) detailed a catalogue of ministerial ineptitude in the sphere of economic planning by Labour ministers supposed to wrest the levers of power from the capitalists.

Moreover, some argued that the strategy was half-hearted; any government seriously wishing to run its economy must resort to full-blown public ownership (Arblaster 1977). However, Keynes was no destroyer; his mission was to restore capitalism with economic homoeopathy, to maintain it against the threatening alternative of communism. He did not advocate heavy-handed intervention, arguing that once aggregate demand reached full-employment level 'there is no objection to be raised against the classical analysis of the manner in which private self-interest will determine what in particular will be produced' (Keynes 1936: 378–9). Yet the bloodstream of capitalism was found to be rich in state-resistant antibodies (Miliband 1961). The instruments of demand management could not function like the remote control of a TV set, producing immediate and reliable results. The state was obliged to cajole rather than command, aiming to make things happen at a distance through the political semaphore of exhortation, rewards and punishments.

Still a ruling class?

Logically opposed to political influence, the capitalists hold the whip hand by generating the wealth required by government (O'Connor 1973). The Crosland belief that the old opposing forces embedded within capitalism had been expunged is part of a general thesis advanced by the anti-Marxist, managerialist school (Burnham 1942). Yet there is strong reason for doubt. From the mid-nineteenth century to the 1970s the proportion of chairmen of major companies from upper-class backgrounds remained constant at 66 per cent (Stanworth and Giddens 1974), their power, through the joint stock company, greater than ever (Scott 1991: 63–92). Behind the world of production there remained the fantasy land of high finance, the City and the Bank of England. This was a world populated by grey pin-striped figures of inestimable influence, fully able, as Harold Wilson was to discover, to rock governments and mock their puny interventions.

From hands off to hands on

According to the theory of demand management, the government could imagine itself the driver of a smooth limousine. A light hand on the steering wheel would avoid the pot-holes along the road and the engine could remain a sealed black box. However, this proved pointless because the engine itself did not seem to be working; governments felt impelled to open the bonnet and get their hands dirty. It was necessary to induce the capitalists to invest and the unions to moderate their demands in a way which would serve the whole economy as well as their own interests. In what has been termed the 'hands-on' stage of Keynesianism, Britain's individualist culture was again to exert its malign influence.

The experience of rivals suggested compellingly that an industrial society with a large working class could not adapt to changing conditions without central direction. However, in Britain the omens were never good. The early success of the industrial revolution produced a blind faith in *laissez-faire* and free trade. The latter doctrine had triumphed over neo-mercantilism at the beginning of the twentieth century and attempts at state-led development by Joseph Chamberlain and Lloyd George had foundered, while Macdonald's National Government had been unable to use its 'doctor's mandate' to cure the economy. Yet a burgeoning literature on corporatism (Lehmbruch and Schmitter 1982) testified that Britain's rivals had shown the way. Acting entrepreneurially, they had become what Dore (1986) terms 'developmental states', running their national economies like great cooperatives.

In Germany, while post-war rhetoric spoke earnestly of the concept of the 'social market' (Shonfield 1965: Ch. 11), governments were more than market referees; they promoted technologies, subsidized lame ducks and pursued regional development (Hardach 1980: 150–204). France was characterized by deep-rooted *dirigiste* traditions and a highly developed bureaucratic ethic of service to a national interest. The *economie concertée* was a form of planning and state intervention in which private companies were embraced in a corporatist *pas de deux*, to be twisted and turned in the community interest. In Sweden, development was eased by a highly cohesive interest group system cementing a large cross-class alliance (Esping-Andersen 1985: 229–35). Most spectactular of all was Japan, where state-directed development miraculously transformed a low-profit economy into an advanced technological leviathan, dominating the world with its high-profit manufactures in automobiles, hi-tech electronics, cameras, chemicals and so on (Magaziner and Hout 1980: 54; Johnson 1982: 318).

British governments made a series of attempts to promote a corporatist approach to the economy. In 1961 the National Economic Development Council (NEDDY) was established to bring together government, unions and employers in a consultative forum. In 1964, under Wilson's 'white heat of technology' rhetoric, a Department of Economic Affairs was created to prise the fingers of the Treasury off the economy. In 1966 an Industrial Reorganisation Corporation (IRC) was established to aid economic adjustment and in 1967 sterling was devalued to boost exports. In 1970 Heath sought to reverse the corporatist trend but his policies collapsed into the ignominy of his notorious U-turns. Throughout, government sought to impose incomes policies, voluntary or statutory according to political climate.

Yet full-blown corporatism was never achieved. All that appeared was what Middlemass (1979) termed a 'corporate bias', a rather loose *pas de trois* in which the dancers came together, touched hands fleetingly, then swirled apart as the music changed. Throughout all the economy continued to languish as stop–go policies, low investment, bad industrial relations, balance of payments crises, rising unemployment, inflation and low morale took their toll. During these frustrating years Heath, embroiled internecinely with the miners, called a general election to demand 'Who governs this country anyhow?' At the conclusion of the campaign he avowed: 'I have no doubt that the real hope of the British people in this situation is that a national Coalition Government could be formed, and that party differences could be put aside until the crisis is mastered' (Young 1990: 90).

However, Heath fell and an alarming sterling crisis saw Britain petitioning the International Monetary Fund for a loan, which was given only on the basis of an anti-welfare deflationary package and the adoption of monetary policy. In 1975 the Labour government established a National Enterprise Board, a more powerful successor to the IRC, and a 'Social Contract' was agreed in which the unions would accept pay restraint in exchange for price controls and improved welfare services. Yet things did not improve and all was ultimately to collapse into the infamous 'winter of discontent' of 1978–9.

Thus the corporate phase had tested to destruction the state's capacity to direct and coordinate the economy. When consensus did not really matter it appeared present, but when it was essential it proved to be a chimera. The failure was caused by the simple fact that all participants remained more concerned with fighting for what they saw as their self-interests. The political culture was such that to do so was entirely acceptable. Union leaders were expected to fight for their members against the bosses (and sometimes other unions), business organizations did likewise and British capital, still hypnotized by the free-trade obsession, continued to flow from the home economy like the holiday-makers forsaking Blackpool to throng the beaches of Benidorm and Torremolinos. Consensus behaviour such as Crosland's revisionism and the Macmillan–Wilson years were depicted as betrayal by many within their parties, and Heath's 'U' entered Conservative demonology, a cautionary tale to be taken very seriously by his successor.

The common sense of decline

British individualist 'common sense' declared that the war of all against all was the only way to run industry. The firm places its responsibility to shareholders above all others. The class system has its very roots in the workplace and supercilious attitudes from bosses confront bloody-mindedness from workers. The British trade union movement remains fragmented, in stark contrast to those of Sweden, Austria and what was West Germany, where confederations of unions are centralized. Dore contrasts British attitudes with those of Japan, where firms see themselves as part of a living community, placing responsibilities to employees (termed 'members'), customers and the local community before those to shareholders (Dore 1986: 214).

The sense of autonomy and jealousy embedded in British industrial culture has been linked to the Glorious Revolution of 1688, which not only sanctified the lord's property in his estate, but also the craftsman's in the mysteries of his trade (Fox 1985: Ch. 4). Olson (1982) argues that Britain's relatively long, smooth constitutional development resulted in an unusually large number of small, special-ized groups, their self-interest unlikely to be congruent with the national interest. They cannot be what he terms 'encompassing groups', such as he finds in Scandinavia.

British trade unions and employers' organizations were formed in the nineteenth century when market liberalism was at its most triumphant. Like firms, they were entitled to make the assumption that they could promote the general good by pursuing narrow self-interest, unions becoming little more than joint stock com-panies for the sale of labour (Currie 1979: 31). The Labour Party, itself established in this divisive culture, could only remain blinkered – a union-driven cart-horse seeking short-term gains for members. The lack of solidarity was most starkly illus-trated in the humiliating collapse of the General Strike in 1926.

Heath, unceremoniously dumped by his colleagues, had left humble origins to head a party of the high and mighty. Despite his failures he had been able, to some extent, to see both sides of the big economic question. His successor had the same credentials, but for her antagonism, punctuated by the clash of swords, was to be the *Leitmotiv*. Thatcher's genius was to recognize and capitalize upon the fragility of the consensus and the shallowness of its foundations. 'No such thing as society' shone like a nugget of 'common sense' in a world of arcane corporatist double-talk.

The silver lining

Yet although the social democratic state fell far short of the ideal, its achievement was by no means negligible. Much consumption had been socialized so that the living standards of millions had been substantially improved. Children no longer went barefoot, or begged on the streets, public sector housing was superior to that offered by private landlords, the nation's children received a sound basic education (to the extent that some were enabled to leave the working class altogether only to bite the hand that had fed their ambition) and, perhaps most significant of all, comprehensive medical treatment was freely available to all. Britain had become a kinder, fairer society, offering a greater sense of personal freedom to ordinary people than ever before.

In so far as there was failure, it was contingent, not cast in the logic of social democracy. In keeping with its hallowed traditions of conservative change, Britain tried to create a peculiar collectivist state by building extensions to the existing liberal one and relying on the old foundations. No self-respecting municipal authority would have granted planning permission for such an enterprise. Yet although the substructure required substantial attention, it was by no means beyond constitutional repair.

Social democracy was more than a legitimating creation of capitalism. Indeed, many capitalists expressed grave reservations about the level of welfare spending, reaching a shrill crescendo in the rise of the New Right, while the left agreed that the capitalist state appeared to have fallen into a 'fiscal crisis' in which it could not pay its way (O'Connor 1973). Indeed, for the right, social democracy was all too successful. The welfare state had so alleviated conditions that people had grown soft, had retreated into a 'post-war funk'. It was time to say enough is enough. In a backhanded tribute to the success of social democracy, the great assault was to be launched.

Hence the new state architects were to come from the New Right, with an approach to constitutional renovation redolent of the methods of explosives expert Blaster Bates. More interested in restoration than reconstruction, they wished only to install a new damp course in the liberal stately home which the tenants (or were they squatters?) had allowed to become dangerously wet.

5 THE THATCHER ASSAULT

Edward Heath had been lampooned by the satirical journal *Private Eye*, his lowly origins mocked with the nickname 'Grocer'. Although after fatal U-turns on economic policy the 1922 Committee closed his shop, in Hollywood style the sequel production was to be 'Daughter of Grocer'. Callaghan's dismal winter of discontent was to be made glorious summer by this daughter of Alderman Roberts, the public-spirited proprietor of a hitherto unsung Grantham grocery undertaking. The state, once inspiration for Plato and Aristotle, was to become a corner shop, its citizens transmogrified eerily into 'customers'. Napoleon's 'nation of shopkeepers' had reached a grotesque apotheosis.

From small acorns

The Conservative manifesto for the 1979 general election did not appear a revolutionary document. Although think-tanks and Sir Keith Joseph had fired some very outlandish New Right broadsides, the ingenue leader of the opposition, mindful of Heath's broken promises, remained guarded. Treated with indulgent contempt by the imperious Callaghan, she trailed in the opinion polls and her remarkably right-wing views were kept well away from the public gaze, and indeed from the gaze of most of her party. Even exposure of her person was parsimoniously rationed by media Svengalis, Gordon Reece and the brothers Saatchi, who did not consider their new product an easy sell.

Yet the ideas were there, in the Thatcher heart, in the hearts of the tree-lined avenues and in the daring papers of the think-tanks. Election victory was to usher them to centre stage in an assault intended to do nothing less than rip up the still shallow roots of British social democracy. It is quite possible in retrospect to speak of the Thatcher assault. As Stuart Hall stressed throughout the era, the assault was more than a set of class-based pragmatic policies; it was a project with hegemonic intent. Thatcher wanted to leave a lasting impression by placing Britain under a new social regime (Hall 1991). The smoking bomb site that was the great cathedral of social democracy testifies to a comprehensive visit by constitutional Cruise missiles as well directed as those that visited Baghdad in 1990. It was a right-wing attack, ironically occasioned by the great slump of world capitalism. Broadly it was held that it was not capitalism that was wrong; social democracy had placed a ball and chain on its ankles.

The key to revival was to roll back the state. From this simple expedient would come freedom for the individual to blossom. The mark of economic revival would be rising profits which would in due course 'trickle down' to all members of the community. Scroungers would be routed as the great welfare state free lunch reached the final course. A comfortable, affluent life-style would accrue only to the deserving and the idle would get a different dessert. According to Thatcher, even God was incensed by scroungers; in 1989, like the stern headmistress to which she was often likened, she reminded the General Assembly of the Church of Scotland that 'If a man shall not work he shall not eat'. Rather than a New Jerusalem the post-war consensus had produced a nation that, like Sodom and Gomorrah, had fallen into ways of depravity.

Minimizing the state

Routing Keynes
While the full extent of the Thatcher assault was not to be discerned from the circumspect manifesto of 1979, the economic solution had been trumpeted as monetarism – a doctrine whereby the state rejects Keynes and all his works and confines itself to nothing more than regulating growth in the money supply (that is, quantity of money in the economy). Ironically, it was the Callaghan government which, in 1976, first adopted the expedient, although with some embarrassment and at the behest of the IMF. For the new government it was to be an article of faith; the crudely meddling hand of government was to be replaced with the sensitive caress of Adam Smith's hidden hand reaching into the twentieth century from the grave.

The lingering Gladstonian ethos meant that when the new government looked to the Treasury it was not faced with the implacable phalanx of pink-shirted Keynesians it had expected. Those Keynesians remaining in the catacombs of the state were hunted like medieval witches (Ponting 1986: 102). Although Permanent Secretary Sir Douglas Wass scorned developments (Young 1990: 156), younger men, if assailed by doubts, kept them beneath pin-striped breasts, accepting a prudential need for Pauline conversion sealed by total immersion beneath the incoming tide. Grovelling mandarins were able to assure Margaret Thatcher 'within six month of taking office that she was surrounded . . . by friends' (Young 1990: 229).

The Treasury had lost much of its traditional authority during the high-spending years of post-war-boom plenty (Heclo and Wildavsky 1974) and the Thatcher revolution promised to restore its former glory. Moreover, the idea of returning to the balanced budget sounded like common sense in the City and the Bank of England, as well as in the corner-shop state.

Unkindly cuts

Another overt target on the Thatcher agenda was public expenditure. Again the process had been reluctantly set in motion by her beleaguered Labour predecessors. Callaghan, as Chancellor of the Exchequer, appeared to be measuring up the corpse of Keynesianism when he announced to the 1976 Labour conference: 'We cannot . . . spend our way out of a recession'. However, Thatcher showed the zeal of an oriental despot; for social democracy it was to be the death of a thousand cuts. Cash limits were imposed with relish throughout the public sector: hospitals, schools and social services departments were soon looking shabby, ill equipped and under-staffed; roads and sewers fell into disrepair; public transport deteriorated and the landscape showed more than ever a public squalor as individualists strove for private affluence. The New Right argued that there could be no free lunches; there were certainly fewer free *school* lunches.

And the lame duck shall walk

The assault was supposed to work an economic miracle. Like a new matron in a ward of malingerers, Margaret Thatcher ended the culture of cosetting industry with government aid, threw open the windows, switched off the life-support machines and drove the patients from their beds. The strategy for survival was Darwinian and would have pleased the shade of Herbert Spencer. The lame were told, if not to take up their beds and walk, at least to stand on their own two feet or, like the heron, learn to perch on one. The alternative was to fall and die. Hardly surprisingly the shock drove many into extinction; the recession of 1979–81 saw manufacturing output collapse by a quarter at a cost of over two million jobs.

Of course the cuts programme was a rather contradictory exercise. The great indus-trial shake-out saved money in aid which promptly went on benefit for the growing pyramid of unemployed. Similarly, council house building cuts were matched with increases in housing benefits paid out. Total public expenditure actually rose in real terms.

The Peter-Paul principle

Cuts in taxes were achieved by robbing Peter to pay Paul. The first Thatcher budget did this in a dramatic way: top-rate income tax was cut from 83 per cent to 60, while the regressive VAT was actually doubled, up to a single rate of 15 per cent. Again the Lawson 'rich people's budget' of 1988 slashed top-rate income tax down to 40 per cent, leaving regressive taxation to rise disproportionately. Only with the blatantly provocative poll tax did the deferential British public begin to smell a rat, yet ironically the easing of the poll tax burden by Chancellor Lamont in 1991, after unprecedented civil protest, was accomplished by raising VAT to 17 per cent. In addition, rate-capping and poll-tax capping broke new constitutional ground. A community was to be denied the right to tax itself – an astonishing interference with liberty.

Yet the failure to achieve the overt goal of less overall taxation did not matter to the New Right; they were undermining the collectivist principle contained in the idea of progressive taxation. What was important was that the rich were paying a smaller proportion.

The great privatization scam

Perhaps the most characteristic aspect of the mission was the rolling back of the frontiers of the state. A collectivist or communal polity is most characteristically displayed in a large state apparatus – 'big government' – so that its dismantling is the most effective symbol of renunciation. Hence the policy encompassed various forms of privatization and quasi-privatization, deregulation, hiving off, opting out, sale of council houses and so on. Broadly, the apologist rhetoric spoke of freedom. It was, however, the highly limited Lockean view of freedom – freedom from the state. The greatest sleight of hand came not merely in the fact of privatization but in its manner. It could have been accomplished by giving shares to their owners, that is, all citizens. In fact, that which belonged to all was sold to the few, the revenue producing tax cuts which would return their money to them! The symbolic message in the sale of the state was never more deeply underscored than in the case of water. The rain which fell upon all, the source of life itself, effectively became the property of a minority.

Of course there is no naturally occurring state–private-sector boundary; the topology of the public sector is politically determined (Hall 1984: 21). The rolling back was largely confined to the economy, the welfare state and that part of the public industrial sector where the sweet odour of profits could be detected. The free economy envisaged by the New Right required a mighty state to maintain law and order (where property must be protected, radical dissent suppressed and industrial relations policed); police pay was dramatically increased and the number of prisons rose.

A necessary corollary of the minimal state is that effective democracy is reduced because less is allocated and controlled in the political sphere. This produced few New Right tears. Indeed democracy, still feared as the 'tyranny of the majority', was reduced in more direct ways.

Minimizing democracy

Too much democracy

Liberal democracy which developed during the nineteenth century was limited democracy. Various means were taken to ensure that serious participation in politics would remain the preserve of the few. The extension of the franchise gave the male masses the vote but little else: unions were impeded in various ways, MPs remained unpaid and the election was effectively restricted to a choice between two competing factions of the political elite.

However, the post-war era viewed the polity in a different light. Not only had the Labour Party become well established by eclipsing the Liberals as the main rival to the hegemonic Conservatives, it had been returned in 1945 with a landslide electoral victory. The working class were also able to enter the gate of the state at various other points. Trade unions joined the decision-making process in a climate of corporatism where they shared power with the representatives of capital and the government itself. Beyond this tripartism there was a general growth in pressure group activity, with numerous organizations fighting for the interests of the underprivileged such as Shelter or Age Concern. At the periphery of the state, the large measure of responsibility given to local government for state welfare meant that working-class councillors could potentially play a direct part in making and implementing local policy. The British state could be said to have opened its doors to the masses, to have become more democratic. Harold Wilson struck fear into establishment hearts by taunting that Labour was the natural party of government, rather like the social democratic parties of Europe.

However, for many in the elevated world of the British establishment it became too democratic; there was much talk of crisis and even a whiff of treason in the air. When Labour returned to office in 1964 hearts fluttered and before long the Lord Chancellor was reduced to taking long drives around Green Park whenever he wished to discuss something in private, believing it 'more than likely that MI5 were bugging the telephones in my office' (Knightly 1968). It was no use his complaining to the Prime Minister because Wilson believed himself to be under surveillance. On 8 May 1968 we are told that newspaper magnate Cecil Harmsworth King secretly met Lord Mountbatten, cousin of the Queen, to discuss the forcible overthrow of the Labour government and the formation of a crisis administration (*The Times*, 7 August 1987).

Establishment pacemakers were set racing in 1974 when the unions, particularly the Scargill-led miners, appeared to bring down the Heath government. For academics and politicians of the right the country was becoming 'ungovernable', the state subject to a kind of political indigestion termed 'overload', its bowels blocked in 'pluralist stagnation'. According to prominent Conservative Lord Hailsham, using the BBC's Reith lecture to disseminate a party message, the constitution had degenerated into an Orwellian 'elective dictatorship'.

Hence, with this background of almost paranoid fear of mass involvement in the polity, it is hardly surprising that a key target in the Thatcher assault was democracy itself. The state was to be sealed off from popular penetration. Government was again to be restored to its nineteenth-century status, as a minority sport for the chosen, rather like grouse-shooting. Legislation was designed to cripple or emasculate the trade unions, end pluralism, curb local government and place more of the state beyond the eyes and ears of democracy.

Union bashing

Not only were state institutions attacked; if they espoused collectivist values, private associations could also come under fire. The need to blacken trade unions in the popular mind was an important strategy. They had to be made *bêtes noires*, transforming the Labour Party's electoral advantage into a liability.

The plans had been hatched while in opposition. New Right acolyte Sir John Hoskyns, a businessman uncovered by Thatcher's early mentor, Sir Keith Joseph, had in 1977 produced a strategic (unpublished) master plan for the elimination of socialism: *Stepping Stones*. This articulated the subterranean longings of hard-core

Conservatives and greatly excited Thatcher (Young 1990: 115). It would not be enough for government to stop talking to trade unions, they should be pole-axed. Jim Prior, one of the Heath men Thatcher was obliged to inherit, resisted, but the 'winter of discontent' forced him to bow to the party hawks. The complex engagement with the unions included epic battles with the steelworkers, railway workers and miners, as well as a legislative assault in which various immunities were removed, secondary picketing outlawed, closed shop laws relaxed and secret ballots designed to allow the inert (often Conservative-voting) mass to curb the radicalism of their leaders.

In a notorious affair, trade unions were banned altogether at the Government Communications Headquarters at Cheltenham. Perhaps most audaciously, the government actually attacked the main opposition party with legislation designed to weaken Labour's financial base in the political levy on trade union members. Despite the libertarian rhetoric, the tactics were redolent of parties with totalitarian designs.

Attacking pluralism: cheques and balances

Another move was a broadside against interest groups in general. The pluralist theory which had become the orthodoxy of the consensus years was decried as leading to profligate spending. Competition between groups, far from producing a system of mutual checks and balances, led to escalating demands which governments were unable and unwilling to combat. Groups had been continually bought off with extravagant policies, increasing the burden on the taxpayer.

The Trades Union Congress (TUC) lost its right to exclusive nomination of members to serve on government consultative bodies and the bodies themselves, including NEDDY, were downgraded or abolished. Government policy was increasingly made on a 'take-it-or-leave-it' basis. The TUC was further undermined as a peak organisation by government willingness to allow breakaway unions a place on consultative forums and various quangos in their own right.

Although the trade unions would no longer sip beer and munch sandwiches at Number Ten, it was also an end to wine and pâté with the CBI, the Institute of Directors, the Bar Council, the Royal Colleges and the BMA. All were to taste some bitter policy dishes with little opportunity to enter the kitchen where they were prepared. However, in these cases, the tasteless roughage served up was designed to restore private profitability through the hidden hand; matron was being cruel only to be kind.

Sealing off the local state

The nature of the New Right agenda was such that local government was bound to be in the front line of attack. It was a vital wheel of social democracy, locked with cogs and drive-belts into its complex mechanism. Politicians' rhetoric was to portray the ordinary people who represented their communities as the quintessence of evil. In the urban areas they were treacherous enemies of the state – the 'loony left'.

It was said that Margaret Thatcher had never forgiven the councillors of Grantham who had voted her father, Alderman Roberts, out of office, and the vengeance to be visited upon their municipal heirs everywhere was to be awful indeed. Cuts bit deeply into all services; deregulation, compulsory competitive tendering, opting out, sale of council houses and privatization sought to weaken authorities by removing functions, threatening to leave them as quaint relics of a bygone age, like well-dressings and parish government. Opposition in the form of the New Urban Left (Boddy and Fudge 1984) roused considerable government outrage; the central grant was reformed continuously to target political opponents, as was rate-capping and the poll tax. In addition, the intention that local authorities become 'enablers' rather than providers meant that a vast array of private firms and voluntary bodies were to be charged with responsibilities for making politically sensitive decisions directly affecting the quality of communal life (Kingdom 1991).

Overall was a relentless pressure from the iron hand of Whitehall. Attempts by local councils to resist were viewed as unconstitutional and a special committee of enquiry was set up to examine the 'politicization' of local government, recommending a battery of restrictions on elected representatives (Widdicombe 1986). Some councillors were taken before the courts for resisting the centre and subjected to crippling surcharges far exceeding the fines imposed upon the most villainous of criminals.

Streamlined to death

There was nothing in the British constitution to say that people could not complain about government policy. There was even a feeling that local representatives of the people could increase democracy through a kind of federal separation of powers. Yet when the New Urban Left tried to resist New Right policies towards local government, Thatcher appeared to know little of such constitutional nicety and the recalcitrants, in the Greater London Council and the metropolitan counties, were blown off the political landscape in a process termed 'streamlining'. This was not merely minimizing the state, it was minimizing democracy, in the most shamelessly naked example of politically motivated constitutional change of the century.

Enlarging the arm's-length state

Traditionally the quango has been seen as fair game for the right, a creature of a leftish tendency, often distributing public largesse beyond the eye of the Treasury. Electoral victory had usually signalled open season. Initially the Thatcher rhetoric made the quango an endangered species but before long the advantages of evading the prying eyes of democracy became pleasantly apparent.

The abolition of the GLC and metropolitan counties saw the genesis of a new hybrid breed of local board to usurp elected local government. So attractive was this that the idea proliferated. The 1985 Transport Act obliged local authorities to hive off their transport operations as separate companies with councillors as only non-executive directors. Reforms to the NHS reduced the already tenuous democratic involvement further by removing councillors from district health authorities, replacing them with businessmen entirely innocent of the ballot box. The policy of opting out for schools and hospitals meant that they were, in effect, to become quangos. The Local Management for Schools initiative also reduced the authority of councillors, being little more than an open invitation for middle-class parents, with a narrow, utilitarian view of education, to take over the schools.

Perhaps the most profligate breeding in the non-elected public sector came from the species Urban Development Corporation (UDC) and its unruly offspring, the 'mini-UDC'. These were controlled by government-appointed business leaders and, with their consumerist theme parks such as Sheffield's Meadowhall and the London Docklands' development, their solutions were to offer more to the yuppie than the homeless and jobless. Similarly, the 1988 Housing Act made provision for Housing Action Trusts to renovate run-down estates; council tenants would be transported to the tender mercies of public–private organizations, set on the disposal of the housing stock to the private sector.

Nor were the central institutions immune to the virus of arm's-lengthism. The *Next Steps* report produced by Thatcher's Efficiency Unit, headed by Robin Ibbs, recommended hiving off parts of the civil service (Jenkins *et al.* 1988). This was to precipitate a plethora of semi-autonomous agencies insulated from ministerial responsibility. The largest section to be so treated was the social security system: some 80,000 civil servants woke up one morning to find themselves employed by semi-autonomous agencies on contract to the government.

The arm's-length state inhabits a marshy terrain between the firm democratic ground of the public sector and the competitive seas of the private one. The shoreline is subject to erosion by voracious waves and it is in peril, like the village of Dunwich, of slipping entirely beneath them, as had most of the industrial public sector by the early 1990s.

Building the state biceps

Although set on reducing the state to anorexic proportions, the government was also concerned to build up its biceps. It is a curious paradox that from the beginning of the 1980s, when the minimalist state became the panacea, the power of the state in general, and that of the Prime Minister in particular, grew increasingly oppressive. Yet this is not really surprising at all; the capitalist state, while calling for economic freedom, must be very strong indeed.

Redefining public administration

'Can do Minister'
It was not enough to re-sculpt the state contours. The attitudes and behaviour of the bureaucrats were also to be assailed. Thatcher's hostility towards civil servants was awesome, predating the rise of the New Right. According to Whitehall legend, within ten minutes of her arrival at the Department of Education and Science in 1970, her Permanent Secretary, Sir William Pile, sensed her 'innate wariness' (Young 1990: 71). Before long she was trying to get him sacked, tearfully explaining to Civil Service Minister Lord Jellico that not only did Pile himself nurse left-wing sympathies, so did his wife! She was to complain petulantly of the loyal mandarin,

who did much for British education: 'It is rather difficult having a permanent secretary who is a security risk' (Young 1990: 72).

The Thatcher approach was to undermine the constitutional notion that civil servants were policy shapers. Instead they were to be seen as 'doers', people who would get on with a job once instructed by their ministerial masters. Any idea that they should question and argue with ministers was anathema. The demand for unthinking obedience was illustrated at the highest level. Cabinet Secretary Sir Robert Armstrong (not constitutionally a prime minister's secretary) seemed willing to go to any lengths, and endure any indignity, to serve his political mistress. As her beleaguered *Spycatcher* trouble-shooter he was mocked in the antipodean courts for his 'economy with the truth', and appeared before the House of Commons Westland Committee to play an obdurately straight bat in defence of the Prime Minister, whose true role in the affair was never to be revealed. The Committee expressed grave concern that so close a confidant of the Prime Minister should at the same time be head of the civil service. A banned BBC programme, *Cabinet*, apparently revealed civil servants achieving grotesque logical contortions in designing a civil defence exercise in which all Conservative and marginal constituencies were safely excluded from direct hit by enemy bombs or fall-out (*The Independent*, 30 August 1988). As a result the Russians were presumed to be directing their main assault on the Cairngorms.

Managing the mandarins

Part of the justification for the assault was the assertion of bad management, a critique based on an idealization of the private sector, the only place where good management existed because only there does the hard discipline of profit bite. Hence the managerialist movement which swept through the public sector was little more than a crude attempt to implant the techniques of the private sector. It was said that Margaret Thatcher saw the state as a corner shop and, in a revealing Freudian veneration for her father, the men brought in were grocers – big grocers. Derek Rayner came from Sainsbury's to scrutinize the civil servants and Roy Griffiths left the busy tills at Marks and Spencer's to conduct major enquiries into the structure and management of the NHS. Sir John Hoskyns (1984: 15) went so far as to argue that the British civil service should receive an injection of up to 400 'high-quality outsiders' from the private sector, although as the economy plunged deeper into recession in the early 1990s some seriously wondered whether British industry had managerial talent to spare on so lavish a scale. Indeed, the managerial reforms were generally outmoded, reflecting the Taylorism of the old Fordist era (see p. 82).

State customers

Good management in the private sector must ultimately be judged according to the profit goal, which is held to entail customer satisfaction – the supreme ethical guide. Throughout the public sector New-Right-speak transformed passengers, subscribers, the old, children at risk, patients, clients, pupils and students into 'customers'. Here was the contractual state as a Platonic ideal, its ethical parameters no different from that of the plumber contracted to fix the kitchen sink. The policy was extended further by John Major, through a kind of customers' code mockingly termed a 'Citizens' Charter' – yet another stick with which to berate state bureaucrats. Yet the individualist culture revealed a low depth of pragmatism, sycophancy and even approval within the state institutions. By the end of 1991 Hall depressingly recorded:

> There is not a school, hospital, social service department, polytechnic or college in the country which has not been so remodelled. The practices of daily life, the professional ethics, the language which is spoken in meetings, the way documents are prepared, work routines designed and priorities defined and fixed, have been totally reframed. (Hall 1991: 11)

Most depressing of all, polytechnic courses in Public Administration, originally intended to create an enlightened social democratic workforce, were renamed 'Public Management' and tutors were obliged to exorcize all reference to the ethical purpose of the state – political philosophy was taboo.

One of us: politicizing the bureaucrats

During the 1980s, with dark symbolism, party sympathy became a means of personal advancement for state employees. The ubiquitous enquiry 'Is he one of us?' rang a sinister note and ensured that 'Yes Men' would occupy key positions. This was largely made possible through the exercise of the colossal patronage power which the British constitution makes available to the prime minister. So extensively was this power used by Thatcher that Hugo Young was able to entitle his definitive work on the virago career *One of Us* (1990).

The appointment of Ian MacGregor, first to head British Steel and then the Coal Board, was particularly symbolic. As a doughty capitalist he waged momentous class-coloured battles with workers in both industries. Of course the right to make also carried a corollary to break. Richard Hoggart spoke of his 'manipulated departure' from the vice chair of the Arts Council (*Observer*, 29 December 1985) and Alasdair Milne, Director General of the BBC, was unceremoniously ejected by Thatcherite chairman of the Board of Governors, Marmaduke Hussey, who appeared to have been appointed to root out suspected left-wing sympathizers within the organization (Milne 1988). In another dramatic intervention, Peter Middleton was brought in as Governor of the Bank of England over the heads of the favoured establishment candidates. Perhaps more insidious was Thatcher's intervention in the matter of top civil service appointments, making the liberal idea of the neutral state increasingly untenable. Head of the Civil Service Sir Ian Bancroft, encouraged to avail himself of the sedentary delights of early retirement in 1981, in order that the faithful Sir Robert Armstrong could add this job to that of Cabinet Secretary, noted how the assumption of such seignorial power by the Prime Minister resulted in a 'grovel count . . . much higher than normal' (Hennessy 1989: 309).

There was also constitutional alarm that, in addition to her command over the Cabinet Office, Thatcher was able to nurture what was a *de facto* prime ministerial department composed of her press office (headed by super-loyal Bernard Ingham), a political office of aides and advisers, and a policy unit of politically committed experts, the heads of which became well-known public figures, including Sir John Hoskyns, Ferdinand Mount, John Redwood and Brian Griffith.

Advice and consent

The autocratic grip over the civil service was strengthened by an increased use of ministerial and prime ministerial advisers and right-wing think-tanks staffed by a curious collection of journalistic and academic eccentrics, such as the Centre for Policy Studies, the Institute of Economic Affairs and the Adam Smith Institute, all rejoicing that their day had come. In addition, there were headline-hitting individuals such as Sir Anthony Parsons (ex-British ambassador to the UN) and maverick economist Sir Alan Walters, who was preferred by the Prime Minister over Chancellor Nigel Lawson in the great political shoot-out in 1989.

The strong arm of the state

The minimal state was minimal only in parts. While hospitals and schools starved, the police force received a massive injection of funds and there was much tough talk of stiffer jail sentencing by the courts and the need to curb antisocial elements in British society. These included pressure groups such as the campaign for Nuclear Disarmament and the National Council for Civil Liberties, where phones were tapped and photographs taken. This was coupled with anti-union legislation which gave the agencies of law and order a greater role in trade disputes and culminated in dreadful clashes between police and workers in strikes such as those involving Britain's miners and print-workers. In addition, the broadcasting media were subject to harassment: various programmes of a political nature were banned; tapes were seized, and programmes were severely criticized (including an interview with a member of the IRA entitled *Real Lives*, a serial by Alan Bleasdale called *The Monocled Mutineer* and a radio series examining the security services entitled *My Country Right or Wrong*), as were interviews with members of an organization held to be opposed to the state – the IRA. BBC reporter Kate Adie was strongly criticized by Conservative Party Chairman Norman Tebbit for her temerity in reporting the US missile attack on Libya (launched from Britain) in non-jingoistic terms. Ordinary people were not immune from the strong arm of the state: the anti-poll-tax demonstrations, bringing millions onto the streets, were not for those of a nervous disposition.

Mind bashing: the hegemonic project

Of course it was not enough for the Thatcher assault to be launched against the institutions. Hers was a mission to the territory of the mind to create a particular common-sense view of the way the world should be, reinforcing the hegemony of the right (see the discussion in Jessop *et al.* 1988). Such common sense was manifest in a variety of ways but at heart was to be an acceptance of an individualist rather than a collectivist view of human nature and of life. The ethos of the cold shower and the open window was not merely to apply to the lame ducks of industry; each individual was to be charged with responsibility for his or her own destiny. Margaret Thatcher never tired of emphasizing how hard she herself worked, while acolyte Norman Tebbit gave the era a catch-phrase by recounting how, when faced by unemployment, his father had jumped on his bike.

This is a fertile emotional ground for the attack on the welfare state. It was the mission of the Thatcherites not merely to remind people of their culpability, but to point out that the social democratic era, with its notions of rights to education, health care and social security, had been pandering to the lazy and indolent to produce a 'dependency culture'. As usual, the ideas were not new; the message was intoned from the nineteenth-century tomb of Samuel Smiles and the prescription was that of Jeremy Bentham who had inspired the savage Poor Law Amendment Act of 1834. It remained surprising that the New Right did not hit upon the workhouse solution to unemployment.

Marketing the miracle

Another key part of the mind assault was the unrelenting mantra implanting the rather hard-to-swallow message that an economic and distributional miracle had occurred. If this was true it could not be said to have rivalled its prototype with the loaves and fishes. On that celebrated occasion the miraculous element lay in the fact that each got a fair share. Perhaps the real Thatcher miracle was that, although it did not happen for the multitude, the multitude remained surprisingly content.

Thus, in an extraordinary irony, the price of the economic miracle (in terms of unemployment, welfare cuts and wage restraint) had been extracted without any justification. Yet this was not an unacceptable compromise for the New Right. Lowering the curtain on social democracy was the real goal. Even without economic recovery, restoring wage differentials, creating a pool of unemployment, stimulating private health care and so on represent pretty good substitutes for economic recovery. The creation of a more socially differentiated society can make the wealthy wealthier in relative terms, can create more of what Hirsch has termed 'positional goods' – those whose allure lies in the fact that others are denied them (Hirsch 1976).

Regardless of the state of the economy, the poor were able to see before their very eyes palpable manifestations of apparent abundance. Thatcherite mores urged the semiotics of success; the rich were told to take pride in their achievements and flaunt the material badges of superiority. The philosophy gave rise to a new species of Homo sapiens, the young upwardly mobile professional, or 'Yuppie'. Builders gentrified areas such as London's docklands for them, tailors droop-suited them, car manufacturers gave them sleek speed machines and Japanese electronics gave them cordless phallic symbols to betoken their virility in restaurants and along the M25. Tim Bell, of Saatchi and Saatchi, the advertising agency which sold the new Conservative Party to the nation, demonstrated his product commitment, declaring: 'I work very long hours, and I like to drive to and from work in a lovely luxurious car. I enjoy being stared at and seeing the car being admired' (Observer, 22 April 1979).

Inducing the losers to admire the winners might be thought a difficult project, even in times of economic buoyancy. To manage the same feat under conditions of persistently low investment, record trade deficits, continuing high unemployment and the return of the grim spectre of inflation required some degree of genius. Those not pocketing the chips in the New Right casino were asked to take comfort in a mysterious 'trickle-down' effect whereby the crumbs descending from the tables of the rich would become progressively bigger, would even contain coatings of jam. Indeed, it is perhaps right to conclude that the key achievement of

Thatcherism is to be found more in the politics of the mind than in the world of reality.

Towards the next frontier

The New Right came to power alleging that capitalism, and British capitalism in particular, had failed not because of its own propensities to crisis, but because of the lead weight of Keynesian social democracy. By 1992, despite the multi-fronted assault, the economy was in as deep a recession as at the beginning of the great experiment. However, in the way that they did not blame the free market in the first place, the New Right denied any suggestion that its own nostrums had failed during the 1980s. It was merely that the attack on the communal state, despite the resolution and zeal claimed for and by Margaret Thatcher, had not been sufficiently radical or far reaching, and further plans were being laid. It would not be fanciful to see the attack going to the extreme lengths of the absolutist libertarians (see Chapter 8). Private prisons were certainly on the agenda and it would not be entirely surprising to find ourselves policed by British Police PLC or an enlarged Securicor. It may prove possible for private individuals to own everything, including the very air we breathe (Demsetz 1967). It is time to explore the New Right mind, to examine the thinking which is said to have set a new political agenda and decimated the British left.

6 THE MYTH OF THE MARKET

It is impossible to underestimate the importance of the concept of the market in British politics; nowhere is the ideology of individualism more purely distilled. It makes more sense here than in any other walk of life, except that the market is not a walk of life; it is an alien wonderland dreamed up by the economists as fantastical as that to which the White Rabbit led Alice. Yet the influence of this thinking is far reaching. The great edifice of liberal theory which underpins the constitution itself has its foundation in a market view of society.

The ideal market

When the New Right litany is intoned, all its verses are underscored by the market drumbeat. It is seen as much more than a means of exchanging goods and services; it is an icon of a faith, a deeply symbolic testimony to the belief that human beings can live without society. Men and women have no responsibility beyond paying their bills, need no love beyond the love of money, and are under no obligation beyond that to the self.

The war of all against all
The market is the denial of any form of communal planning, producing outcomes which are the results of a myriad small decisions made by individuals having no thought for the well-being of one another. Indeed, it goes further than this; individuals are expected to do each other harm through a process of unrelenting competition. Life is truly a war of all against all and Hobbes was certainly aware of

the market society when he outlined his inhospitable vision of social existence (see p. 10).

However, the joyous paradox uncovered by the classical economists is that the outcome of the battle is no Hobbesian nightmare but the best that could possibly happen – the greatest happiness for the greatest number. In fact economists prefer the word 'utility' (invariably measured in terms of money) to 'happiness' and if, as the old proverb insists, this does not really equate with happiness, it is warmly regarded as a satisfactory surrogate. In the market-place maximization is the key to behaviour: consumers maximize utility and producers maximize profit. The result of this is a great harmonious outcome – the optimum allocation of resources, a wondrous 'spontaneous order'.

The price is right

Within the market, the all-important pivot is the price mechanism, a giant information processor, subtly adjusting to all changes in technology and consumer preference and ensuring that the right amount of each commodity is produced, in the right place and at the right price. At the end of the day there is always a price which miraculously matches supply with demand; no one is left unsatisfied and each transaction had added to the sum of human happiness. In the complexity of the modern economy no central authority could possibly allocate resources with the same precision or flexibility. The market spontaneously utilizes the entire sum of human knowledge.

What of questions of social justice? It is argued that the market cannot be unfair because it is a neutral machine, unable to make value judgements or show preferences. On the other hand, it follows a stern morality, rewarding effort and punishing sloth. This idea was sublimely enticing to members of the Victorian establishment, leaving them secure in the knowledge that the poverty and suffering counterpointing their astonishing accumulation of wealth were all part of a natural system of justice.

The apostles

While the prophets of the eighteenth and nineteenth centuries had been lionized, the post-war apostles were thrown to the lions of the welfare state consensus. Yet like Christians in the catacombs they were determined to keep the flame of truth alight; their evangelic fulminations against the decadence of deficit financing and the idolatory of the false god Keynes displayed a religious fervour.

Perhaps the greatest apostle was Friedrich Hayek (1899–1992), who witnessed in his long lifetime the horrors of both fascism and Stalinism. It is not surprising that most of his writing was preoccupied with the dark threat to liberty posed by the state. He saw social justice as a mythical holy grail and would even limit suffrage on the paradoxical grounds of defending democracy (Hayek 1982: Vol. III, 138). He consistently displayed a profound hostility towards all public bureaucratic life-forms and any variant of liberal democracy.

Hayek was to perpetuate a body of thought originated by neo-classical economist Carl Menger (1840–1921) at the end of the nineteenth century (dubbed the Austrian School). This developed the deeply influential marginal utility theory of value which challenged the labour theory of value. Another member of the school was Ludwig von Mises (1881–1973), who stressed the impossibility of state planning. Hayek sought to combine this essentially empirical body of theory with a wider philosophical mission to provide an apologia for modern capitalism which he believed to be the *sine qua non* of the free society. However, although the Austrian School fundamentally opposes goals such as equality, redistribution and the idea of social justice, it does admit a limited role for the state in offsetting social hardships.

Importantly, Hayek did not see the individual as omnipotent in rationality; ignorance, imperfect knowledge and limited ability are very much present. However, the market resolves the uncertainty; the 'spontaneous order' is the outcome of human action but not of human design. Indeed, the processes are beyond understanding; veneration of the market is truly a kind of faith, not to be justified entirely in rational terms.

Although differing in certain respects, Hayek's work is frequently coupled with that of Milton Friedman (1962) and the Chicago School, who stress the link between the market and politics under the dominant thesis that it will automatically promote political freedom and democracy. Friedman is a staunch advocate of the economic policy known as monetarism, which calls for a freeing of markets from Keynesian-style intervention.

The apostles were to find a high priestess worthy of their message. Through right-wing think-tanks and the appointment of ministerial advisers, journalists and academics previously considered eccentric were to be heard in the highest courts of the land. Their fundamentalist faith was to become part of the common sense which pervaded the consciouness of a nation that was as proud to be the home of Marks & Spencer as of Hobbes and Locke. The gospels were to provide a legitimating superstructure for the renowned Thatcher instincts, to be expressed with unshakable conviction (Young 1990: 212).

Stranger than fiction: the imperfect market

While it is true that nobody's perfect, the extent to which the real world falls short of the 'perfect market' of theory gives pause for considerable thought. Its individualism is of a very special kind, knowing nothing of a person's intrinsic worth, integrity, compassion or talents. Although 'supreme', *Homo economicus* is a cardboard cut-out, a one-dimensional man. This lonely figure does not even appear to have a mate, for the arcane theories make no mention of *Femina economica*. In fact, he is an entirely fantastical being, like Frankenstein's monster, energized in the laboratory by the thunder and lightning of the imagination.

Equally fictitious is his world, the textbook terrain of perfect competition, based upon small-scale production, perfectly informed actors, little state involvement, each actor owning land and property, labour not seen as a commodity, and free trade in an unprotected world economy governed by economic laws working with the precision and regularity of gravity. There are no real ethical objections to this vision, indeed Marx described it as 'a very Eden'. Yet the more we compare the map of this world with reality, the more we must doubt its value as a guide.

What of the invigorating competition extolled by New Right politicians and economists (neither of whom are obliged to live by its cathartic logic)? The love of

competition appears rather like the declaration of a cad, professed more than practised. Contrary to theory, most economic actors abhor competition as much as nature
does a vacuum. The real world economy is replete with devices designed to confound
the market and reduce its uncertainty, including agreements with suppliers, controlled prices, cartels, monopolies, cross-subsidies and much *bogus* competition (as
when chocolate bars bearing 'competing' brand names are disgorged from the intes-
tines of a single giant conglomerate).

Even the idea that the free market is inhabited by individuals is false. The dominant players on the stage are associations, increasingly multinational companies with
more corporate power than governments and able to dictate to them, influencing
them over when to raise interest rates, when to form alliances, how to vote in the UN,
and when to send their young people to their deaths under the sophisticated
weaponry with which they supply the world.

Milton Friedman deals with this criticism by denying the real existence of corporations, arguing that the term serves merely as a 'figurative' intermediary
between stockholders and employees. 'Only people have incomes and they derive
them through the market from the resources they own' (Friedman and Friedman
1980: 40). Not only is this supposed to answer any criticism of corporate power, it
enables him to treat state restrictions on corporations as interference with the liberty
of individuals. Yet, curiouser and curiouser, the logic stands on its head when it
comes to trade unions; here the New Right finds state limitation vital.

Far from relishing the rigours of the market, industrialists are themselves more
than ready to be suckled at the breast of the state, assiduously lobbying for subsidies
and other benefits (Beer 1982: 75). Thus, for example, haulage companies are
excused the cost of maintaining the road network which their juggernauts merci-
lessly destroy, while the more ecologically friendly competitor British Rail must add
track maintenance to its own costs.

The perfect market is the epitome of individual rationality. Decisions are characteristically based upon a careful weighing of information on prices, costs, forecasts,
demand levels and so on. In reality most economic actors operate in a state of blinkered confusion and entrepreneurs will often boast of their intuition (or if they are
more honest, their luck) in striking the deals that made their fortunes. The costs of a
truly rational decision would be quite prohibitive. The family of a rational parent
would starve, entrepreneurs would never launch new products and no one would buy
petrol for fear that the filling station around the corner would offer a larger free glass
goblet. Thus the precise machine is no more than a great game of roulette. Ironically,
entrepreneurs tacitly acknowledge this when asked to justify profits, describing them
thrillingly as the rewards of risk.

To the economists of the textbook world the market is a great game of cricket
played according to the rules by English gentlemen. Yet, from great City scandals
such as the Guinness affair, a symbol of the 1980s, to the back-street second-hand-
car transaction, the process is one of tense psychology, brinkmanship, double-talk
and dubious morality. In the real world self-interest goes beyond formal market roles
to include lies, deceit, backhanders, dubious promises, industrial espionage, sweet-
eners, uneasy coalitions, shady transactions and insider deals, all to collapse in
betrayal, turncoatism and so on. Moreover, the business class does not confine its
meetings to boardroom and shop floor; encounters also take place in the shadowy

world of the London club, the yacht club and the Freemasons' lodge. Here they will rub well-tailored shoulders with leaders from other bastions of society: the police force, Whitehall and Conservative Central Office. The market will be as free as they wish it to be.

One of the market's greatest claims is its ability to allow customer choice, to promote the 'consumer sovereignty' said to be superior to the constitutional sovereignty bestowed through the ballot box. Yet under advanced capitalism, the so-called sovereignty is undermined at numerous points by the biggest industry of all, one which does not actually produce anything capable of being eaten, worn or lived in. The billion-pound advertising industry is devoted to the shaping of minds, controlling our wants and attitudes in accordance with what industries find it most profitable to produce. Like the disreputable travelling medicine salesman of old, with dubious potions and cure-all nostrums, the advertisers persuade us what to drink, what to eat, what to wear and how to smell. Indeed, we are instructed to destroy our health with tobacco, alcohol, junk food and tooth-rotting soft drinks. Which consumer ever used his sovereignty to demand flaccid chips, on cardboard plates, to be eaten with flimsy cutlery while seated upon a cold, immovable plastic seat?

A fundamental myth is that the free market is self-regulating, tending towards stability. In reality it is notoriously prone to crises and breakdowns and, as Keynes pointed out, is moved by mercurial psychological forces. Thus, for example, the level of investment is a function of capitalists' intuitions about the future (ironically Hayek makes much of our inability to make forecasts). They watch each other for signs, and pessimistic thoughts can soon escalate into loss of confidence and panic, producing a real downturn, a slump, and unemployment for thousands of innocent bystanders. Repudiation of the idea of self-regulation comes from the profoundly logical brain of the father of cybernetics, Norbert Weiner, who calls the idea 'simple minded'. 'There is no homeostasis whatever. We are involved in the business cycles of boom and failure, . . . in the wars which everyone loses' (Weiner 1965: 159). The mysterious hidden hand envisaged by Adam Smith does not soothe, rather it delivers a sharp blow to the solar plexus.

Finally there is the hairspring of the elegant market clockwork, the delicate price mechanism connecting buyers and sellers to their mutual advantage. The miracle occurs without affection, 'without requiring people to speak to one another or to like one another' (Friedman and Friedman 1980: 32). Though presented *ad nauseam*, this suggestion of justice is wickedly bogus. The preferences expressed through the mechanism reflect resources not needs; demand is defined as desire plus ability to pay. The real world market is an auction where some of the bidders are dumb; they could starve without demanding bread.

Does truth matter?

The accusation that their world is an elegant fiction is shrugged off by the theorists (especially Friedman) with the cavalier declaration that veracity is unimportant; all that matters is the value of the predictions (and prescriptions) generated. This flies in the face of the Euclidean, logico-deductive method (supposedly the basis for the reasoning), where axioms are self-evident truths. For example, if in Euclid the shortest distance between two points were shown not to be a straight line then the whole edifice of deduction from such a premiss would necessarily collapse.

Moreover, the members of the Austrian School go well beyond the idea that all goods and services are justly cleared by the market to monumental claims that it underpins the whole edifice of democracy and freedom, that it is the only ethical basis for life. The auctioneer and second-hand-car salesman replace the philosopher and priest in the great scheme of things. Or do they?

The market and the great scheme of things

As a bedrock of their thinking liberals argue that the market is in some way natural; that is, it would be found in a mythical state of nature (see Chapter 2). Hence the New Right logic is rather like that of the pig Squealer in *Animal Farm* who proclaimed: 'four legs good, two legs bad'. The modern squealers assert with equal conviction: 'market good, state bad'. The market is said to promote freedom, democracy and, ultimately, the common good. How valid are the grand claims? This is the question for the rest of this chapter.

The market as nature intended

Chapter 2 showed that Locke believed the market to exist in a state of nature. This monumental assumption is challenged in Chapter 8. Here we consider the extent to which the market is really a natural part of life. New Right rhetoric implies no limit to the scope of the market, no places where it may not insinuate its beneficent presence. It does not take much argument to demonstrate the absurdity of such a notion.

In the first place, although labour is a commodity in the market it is not produced by such means. Rather it is reproduced and maintained in working order by special machines termed women, operating within a factory known as the family. Women give birth, rear children, and care for their husbands on the basis not of a fee, but of love and duty. Although children usually demand high rates for car-washing, a mother charging for meals and lodging would be regarded as inhumane, and one applying market criteria to sex would fall foul of the law on male conjugal rights. There are other ways in which human reproduction ignores the logic of the market: parents do not regulate their fecundity according to the labour market, resulting in a permanent demand/supply mismatch (Hodgson 1984: 70).

In a slave economy some people actually buy and sell others. Logically, this is another area where the New Right could extend the principles of possessive individualism. Schools could own their pupils and sell them to employers; parents could own their children and do likewise. However, this arrangement is not welcome under capitalism, where it is labour, not people, which is seen as the commodity, and those buying can disclaim all responsibility for the persons in whom the labour is vested.

Do we rely entirely on market morality? To a great extent it might appear that the market dispenses with moral considerations altogether. We can do what we can afford to do, and we have no right to attempt it by any other means. Hence it is not immoral to reduce people who have invested their lives in the development of a skill to poverty by replacing them with machines. However, whether or not we could afford to, we could not read, say, *Last Exit to Brooklyn* until a judge decided so in the swinging sixties. Although the home of individualism, Britain retains a set of highly uptight moral values. The Victorian era is not only renowned as the free-market high spot, it is a byword for narrow puritanism. While British tourists stare goggle eyed at the sex industries of the US, Australasia and Europe, they experience an atmosphere of non-marketized puritanism at home. While a doctor may charge for the kiss of life, the idea that a women should charge for sex is anathema.

Another area excluded from competition is that of the natural monopoly; some industries involve such a heavy investment of capital that competition by several firms would obviously be wasteful of the nation's resources. Hence there has long been agreement that certain industries represent 'natural monopolies' which should be allowed to stand outside the market but subject to some form of state control, replacing the discipline of competition either by nationalization or regulation.

Whether or not it is true that the best things in life are free, a wide range of goods and services are not easily seen as tradable commodities. At the most basic level there are sunlight, fresh air and water. Beyond this there are what economists term 'public goods' (street lighting, street cleaning, roadworks and an elusive commodity, information), which the market will not provide because it is virtually impossible to levy a charge, since non-payers cannot be easily excluded from enjoying the service.

The market also knows nothing of the concept of the gift, by definition a non-market transaction. There are numerous gift relationships within a society, from telling someone the time to donating blood. Gifts provide an outlet for a range of human feelings from altruism to duty, and it would be difficult to imagine society without them. The welfare state can itself be seen as an institutionalized system of gift relationships (see p. 108).

It is a curious paradox that while free-market theorists expect firms to behave competitively, they do not advocate such behaviour *within* the firm. This was one of Adam Smith's key insights; it was cooperation, through division of labour, rather than competition, which would raise production to undreamed-of heights. More-over, where division of labour operates, workers do not trade half-finished products with each other. One man does not sell a chassis to another who attaches the wheels, and so on (Coase 1937); all is coordinated by managers. The firm, like the family, is a subversive command economy lying at the heart of the market.

Finally, although advocates claim ubiquity for the market, far from wanting to embrace all, it is an exclusion mechanism. Although poverty is a necessary part of a system energized by rewards and penalties, *pour encourager les autres*, the market has nothing to offer those with empty wallets. In the casino only those with chips can play the games.

Who draws the boundary?
Clearly the idea that the market can entirely permeate life is absurd. Even so, the New Right determined to place as much as possible in this sphere by privatizing the natural monopolies, inventing ways of overcoming the problem of public goods

(toll roads can exclude non-payers, contracting can make local taxes a charge levied by private providers), and the curious device of the internal market for public bureaucracies whereby colleagues sell their services to each other. In 1988 Chancellor Nigel Lawson boasted to the Adam Smith Institute: 'We have privatised nearly 40 per cent of the state commercial sector . . . By the time the present programme is complete, some 60 per cent will be in private hands' (Treasury press release, 27 July 1988). Such statements underline an essential point in our analysis: the precise boundary between market and non-market is no naturally occurring great barrier reef; it is determined by nothing more than political decisions.

The big market and the small state

A central claim for the market is that it is enacted in an area beyond the state – 'civil society'. It is from this line of logic that we hear the claim for *laissez-faire*, for 'minimal government'; the state is merely a 'night watchman', warming his idle hands against the silent brazier.

Historical evidence mocks the minimalist thesis. The society of Hobbes's time was witnessing the emergence of a possessive free market but it was not a *laissez-faire* system. Extensive state regulation was required, the great bulk of it designed to reduce market fluctuations and protect the social order from the disruptions induced by the market (Macpherson 1962: 62). The subsequent development of capitalism saw the trail blazed and kept open through a colossal increase in continuous, centrally directed, state intervention. Creating Adam Smith's economic universe was an immensely complex enterprise. Polanyi notes how the introduction of free markets, 'far from doing away with the need for control, regularisation and intervention, enormously increased their range. Administrators had to be constantly on the watch to ensure the free working of the system' (1957: 141). Enclosure Acts, canal, railway and turnpike Acts, various banking Acts and Companies Acts sculpted the economic landscape. A host of private Acts paved the way for the rise of the all-important *ad hoc* local bodies and municipalities as nineteenth-century capitalism created modern local government (Kingdom 1991: 20–31).

Modernizing the state

It is the importance of the state to capitalism which explains why the emergent bourgeoisie hijacked the institutions of old and revamped them to serve their special purposes. No constitutional stone was left unturned in a period which saw nothing less than the creation of the modern state. The Victorian men of business preferred modestly to conceal their power behind the minimalist state rhetoric, but it was minimalist only to the extent that its drive-belts and cog-wheels kept from under the nimbly moving feet of the profit accumulators.

Facilitating the economic order

A second reason why the free market cannot dispense with the modern state lies in its endemic tendency to run into trouble. The market has only one thing in common with true love: it does not run smooth. Indeed, left to itself it has lurched blindly from one crisis to the next and when this happens only the state can pick up the pieces. These crises included overproduction (or lack of demand), unemployment, rising production costs, unacceptable externalities (damage to the environment), loss of confidence, rising labour costs and infighting within the capitalist class. The breathtaking leaps of capitalism, although seeming effortless and unsupported, are like those of the sequinned ballerina, only possible with a muscular partner who stays out of the spotlight, lifting her so that she soars and supporting her when she falters.

The market and freedom

The idea of freedom lies at the very heart of liberal thinking. Locke imagined a state of nature in which each individual was autonomous and unfettered and saw the state as a violation of this. Yet he was no anarchist; nature had its inconveniences and the state was necessary to secure 'life, liberty and estates'. On the other hand, he saw the market as part of nature and therefore an expression of natural freedom which the state must protect. Thus there is a sense in which the state represents an advance on a state of nature, but things must not be allowed to go too far. Hobbes believed it necessary to forgo a great deal of freedom, but liberals follow Locke in arguing that the sacrifice is basically undesirable and should be kept to a minimum.

The free-marketeers go on to argue that the market, as an expression of freedom, will, if allowed to flower, guarantee further freedoms: the freedoms of movement, expression and so on which make a civilized life possible. However, the claim is dubious on the grounds of logic. The idea that the capitalist bourgeoisie will wish to guarantee freedom to the masses does not square with Marx's fearsome prediction that the working class would ultimately revolt against their exploiters. A capitalist free-market state wishing to arrest this historical career towards catastrophe is required to maintain inequality in wealth and power while at the same time containing the resultant social tensions – a difficult balancing act, which is unlikely to be accomplished by bestowing too much freedom on the masses. How far does the British experience support the freedom via the market thesis?

Freedom of the person: watch your step

From the first the bourgeoisie required the state to safeguard its members from the social and economic risks they were taking at home and in the colonies abroad. It is by no means insignificant that Peel's Metropolitan Police Act came six years before the Municipal Corporations Act of 1835. The state ensured a passive labour force by policing the industrial cities and maintained the trade routes by policing the world. In the 1980s the repressive forces of the state were refurbished and unleashed against striking miners, dockers and print-workers, as well as unemployed inner-city rioters and anti-poll-tax demonstrators. In particular, Britain's young black population felt particularly threatened by the forces of the state and charges of racism within the police force were rife. Indeed, individualist theory has difficulty with ethnic minorities since they constitute a group, and groups are anathema. Moreover, policies to assist minorities, such as positive discrimination, are held to violate the rights of other individuals (see Kymlicka 1989).

Freedom of association: watch your company

A brief examination of the history of British trade unionism dispels any roman-ticized notion that free-market capitalism welcomes free association. The grim spectre of the French Revolution conditioned establishment attitudes to radical action and the rise of the organized left is a story of bitter struggle. During the New Right era, the government did not merely turn deaf ears to the union voice in matters of policy, it fired a fusillade of repressive legislation (see p. 49).

Freedom of speech: mind your tongue

Britain probably has the most secretive state in the world. While others have Freedom of Information Acts, we have Official Secrets Acts. There have been battles royal over the right of ministers to allow the public to know what happens in government by publishing memoirs, and the *Spycatcher* affair presented an aston-ished world with a farce worthy of the home of Gilbert and Sullivan. When it questions the pro-market case, free speech is also jeopardized, with the media particular targets. The 1980s saw the BBC under sustained pressure for alleged left-wing bias (see p. 54). Not only were Thatcherites brought into controlling positions and the Director General sacked (see p. 53), but in 1988 a Broadcasting Standards Authority was set up under a doyen of the establishment, ex-editor of *The Times*, Sir William Rees-Mogg. Genuine liberals saw this as little more than a form of censorship (Brittan 1988). The press, being largely in the ownership of enthusiastic free-market proponents, is seen as less of a problem. Moreover, their dependence on advertising creates added pressure on what they will say. Indeed, free speech could be taken to mean the right of the right to say what it thinks right.

Freedom in morality: sad to be gay

The nineteenth-century high point of market freedom was counterpointed with a legendary puritanism. (For the upper classes this was not exactly true in that the oldest profession, in which children as well as thousands of impoverished women were engaged, was a growth industry to rival cotton or heavy goods manufacture.) The Thatcher era heard much rhetoric of returning to Victorian standards and values, with a penchant for a rigidly hierarchical authoritarian society. The 1960s had seen a general relaxation in restraints (symbolized in the *Lady Chatterley* trial and the widespread availability of easy contraception), developments which were castigated by the New Right. Norman Tebbit spoke sneeringly of 'the era and attitudes of post-war funk which gave birth to the permissive society', and the new climate provided an opportunity for a miscellany of moral crusaders such as Mary Whitehouse (sex on TV), Victoria Gillick (sex and the young), homophobics (Clause 28), anti-abortionists (the 18-week bill), and hangers (supported by Margaret Thatcher). This is the uptight moral environment in which the highly competent Director of Public Prosecutions is forced to resign (as happened in 1991) for kerb-crawling.

Academic freedom: mind what you think

Academic freedom is not a special luxury or privilege of university professors, it is a fundamental principle with deep implications for the health and rationality of a society. Genuine modern liberals such as Rawls (1973), Raz (1986) and Dworkin

(1984) would argue that a society must offer the right of choice not only in the restricted universe of the market but over all aspects of life. Free questioning should be permitted to explore the validity of fundamental beliefs about the nature of the good life itself. However, a free-market society, with its inbuilt tendency towards inequality, is particularly vulnerable to such criticism and will not encourage it.

Hence schools, colleges and universities came under siege during the 1980s. Philosophy professors and others were chided for not teaching 'relevant' disciplines, security of tenure for university lecturers was ended, local authorities were attacked for introducing subjects such as 'Peace Studies', student grants were frozen and the new Core Curriculum was introduced to restrict the professional right of teachers to judge what to teach. Education Secretaries and the Prime Minister stressed that history teaching should be essentially British and patriotic in order to discourage scepticism amongst the young.

Freedom to be free
Here is a freedom which gives the market considerable difficulty: the freedom to participate fully in the normal life of the community. The Beveridge Report spoke of freedom from want, disease, ignorance, squalor, idleness and so on. Such freedoms do not come from the minimalist state, they must be positively conferred *by* the state. Because they tend towards greater equality they are opposed by the free-marketeers, who venerate inequality as a spur. Yet when these freedoms are denied, the others become hollow rhetoric: the right to free speech is little comfort to the sick who can only groan their agony, and free assembly is cold comfort to the homeless.

Freedom to possess
The idea that the market is natural is based on the axiom that the freedom to own a piece of God's earth is itself natural; Locke considered people's property to be as rightfully theirs as their limbs. Hence possession is indeed a key freedom in an individualist, market-based society – the one supreme right upon which all other are said to depend. Yet, paradoxically, asserting the primacy of property logically curbs other freedoms. Locke's initial view of the right to possess might seem self-evidently justifiable in a land of abundance where all can possess equally. However, in the context of a capitalist society, the right becomes a means for some to possess in gross abundance so that others are denied. 'These freedoms to use or dispose [of property], . . . under capitalism, generate a matching set of unfree-doms, whereby non-owners are precluded from either using or disposing' (Heald 1983: 60).

Curate's egg freedom
Hence we must conclude that, far from guaranteeing the widespread freedoms applauded by liberals in the humane tradition of J. S. Mill, the individualist, marketized society logically demands quite the opposite: a free market demands a strong state (Gamble 1988). By the end of the 1980s few British citizens could feel a sense of greater freedom from the state. Indeed, for many Thatcher supporters, her domineering image captured the spirit of a new age of 'resolution'. Stuart Hall aptly characterized the style as 'authoritarian populism' (Hall 1980). Under the

unfettered market, liberal democracy appears as a kind of constitutional curate's egg, liberal only in parts.

The market and democracy

It is argued from the right that the kind of freedom required by capitalism provides a particularly benign ecosystem for democracy.

> Historical evidence speaks with a single voice . . . I know of no example in time or place of a society that has been marked by a large measure of political freedom, and that has not also used something comparable to a free market to organise the bulk of its economic activity. (Friedman 1962: 9)

However, Marx's essential point is that capitalism creates private power which actually overrides the democratic system. Hence, the fact that democratic institutions prevail where one finds the market does not mean that they are effective; they may be cultivated merely as window dressing or legitimation needed to allow the market to have its inegalitarian way. People are led to believe they enjoy the status and dignity of noble Athenians, while in reality they are ruled by tyrants in boardrooms and banks – hence Lenin's jibe that liberal democracy was 'the best possible shell' for capitalism.

How effective are the British democratic institutions? At the outset we find that the very culture exudes non-democratic vibrations. 'Suspicion of democratic procedures, hostility to democratic pressure, the fear of democratic control, are to be found in all parts of society' (Miliband 1984: 28). The industrial revolution induced no inrush of democratic air. The bourgeoisie recognized the extension of the franchise as a necessary step to complement their growing economic power with the political power which would make the state a more efficient vessel for their enterprise. What they wanted was a slice of the parliamentary cake for themselves, not for the masses. They proved as anxious as the landed grandees they challenged to resist radical pressure from below, bitterly disappointing their working-class supporters in their 1832 Reform Act.

Far from being welcomed as the natural complement to the free market, democracy was feared. After the 1867 Reform Act had extended the franchise to the urban male working class, political commentator Walter Bagehot agonized over the likely surge of the barbarians through the portals of the state: 'a political combination of the lower orders . . . is an evil of the first magnitude, . . . would make them supreme in the country . . . So long as they are taught not to act together, there is a chance of this being averted' (Bagehot 1963: 277). Although the franchise was extended, parliamentary democracy was merely a Tweedledum–Tweedledee choice between competing factions of the old elite. Moreover, a special theory of representation was outlined by arch conservative Edmund Burke, emphasizing not the supremacy of the will of the people, but the *independence* of MPs from their constituents.

Today ordinary MPs have but negligible influence over the affairs of state; party dominance makes them lapdogs. The legislative process, Question Time and the activities of the scrutiny committees are but charades, while the primitive, first-past-the-post electoral system makes Parliament a crazy hall of mirrors reflecting the nation in grotesque caricature. Parliamentary supremacy means in effect the supremacy of a prime minister elected by a tiny proportion of the nation.

Liberal democracy: limited democracy?

It is clear that the strain of democracy which has flourished since the nineteenth century in Britain falls short of any Athenian idyll. In the late 1970s Nicos Poulantzas charted the progress of a new kind of authoritarian movement whereby western democracies which had developed an intensive degree of state control in social and economic life saw a decline in their democratic institutions (Poulantzas 1978: 203). The Thatcher assault of the 1980s could leave little doubt that democracy was crippled in many significant ways.

Why then do right-wing politicians and intellectuals set such store by the idea that the free market is intimately wedded to democracy? The answer lies in the notion of liberal democracy, the particular, oxymoronic, designer variant of the real thing. Liberal democracy comes to mean, not freedom *for* democracy, but freedom *from* democracy.

The market and the commonweal

Finally comes this most crucial justification of the market: the belief that it conduces the common good by the operation of the hidden hand.

The rich get richer and the poor get poorer

Through the market the rich can consolidate their position through property ownership, access to elite education and so on, to become even richer. Inequality is a necessary and deliberate outcome. How can this be supported on the utilitarian grounds of the common good? The ingenious answer lies in the magical 'trickle-down' effect: the way to help the poor is to make the rich richer. This incentive encourages them to such exertion that the economy kick starts into renewed life. However, the recession of the early 1990s, coming after the lavish largesse of upper-bracket tax cuts, offered ample refutation of the thesis. In April 1990 the government confessed that the income of the bottom 10 per cent had risen at only half the national average (*Observer*, 8 April 1990).

Inequality cannot further the common good; on the contrary, it harms it. The problem goes beyond the fact that we are not all free to dine at the fabled Dorchester Hotel. If people have unequal access to certain fundamental services such as health care and education, then the whole society is impoverished and endangered. It was the logic of this which enabled Edwin Chadwick to promote his vital public health reforms in the nineteenth century. He pointed out that the germs cultivated in the lungs of the working class, unaware of the divinely ordained class system, would invade the delicate nostrils of the bourgeoisie, even of royalty. However, Chadwick and the utilitarians did not realize that the virus of inequality could also ravage the whole fabric of society. If the rich monopolize the best education there can be no expectation that the finest brains will work in the key areas of science, the arts, medicine, technology and even business.

Although it is no problem to the 'no such thing as society' school of ethics, inequality fragments the community, promoting the two-nations mentality which impoverishes social life. Not only are the poor forced to suffer materially and emotionally, they experience erosive feelings of envy. At the same time the wealthy, even if they are not made uneasy by their consciences, must live in perpetual fear of revolt by the have-nots.

The Prisoners' Dilemma

The Prisoners' Dilemma is a well-known game illustrating the folly of believing that individualism produces the optimum result. Two malefactors are arrested for a crime which they have committed together. Each is placed in a separate cell and given the option to own up or remain silent. They are also told that if both confess each will receive five-year sentences, but if only one owns up he or she will receive only one year while the silent accomplice suffers a ten-year stretch. Alternatively, if both remain mute, they will each get two years. Reasoning as individualists they realize that remaining silent would carry the grave risk of ten years, so they confess, gaining the more favourable options of one or five years. Hence they get five years each, yet with the mutual trust to remain silent both would have been better off. Alternatively, with access to a good lawyer, they could have been guided by advice based upon knowledge of the whole picture.

This little fable resembles many typical situations in communal and political life. People act in what they believe to be their individual self-interest to produce not a spontaneous order, but an outcome which is worse for all, including themselves, a paradox discussed in much greater detail by Elster (1983).

The Tragedy of the Commons

This simple fable illustrates the problem of self-interested behaviour in a community by reference to a group of herdsmen with common grazing rights over a piece of land. Rational self-interest would decree that each will introduce as many cattle as possible, even beyond the point of overgrazing. The cost of each new animal is shared by all while the benefits accrue to the individual owner. Even if they are aware that this behaviour will lead all to lose their livelihoods, they are powerless as individuals to avert the imminent tragedy. Again, the only answer is someone with an overview, who will advise individuals to subjugate their egos to the greater good.

The free market and the economy

Free-marketeers reject reasoning of this kind, arguing that the free market is good for the national economy. However, to do so they must go backwards rather than forwards in time. The great days of empire are invariably invoked to capture the romantic potential of the market, when free trade made Britain the workshop of the world. However, as was argued in Chapter 4, the story of the British economy since the mid-nineteenth century has been one of continual decline, outstripped by rivals practising various forms of state-led adjustment and repudiating the idea that self-serving businessmen would automatically do the right thing (see p. 40).

In the unmanaged British economy entrepreneurs stuck to traditional manufactures instead of developing new technologies which were to make the running in the twentieth century. Like the decisions of the two prisoners, those of the investors and entrepreneurs were entirely rational according to the free-market, self-interest maxims of Smith. However, they were woefully irrational for the community as a whole (Marquand 1988: 121–3). Only the state, playing the part of the good lawyer, can take the overall view and deduce the really rational behaviour.

Moreover, a free trade *idée fixe* saw British businessmen more prone than others to establish, or become part of, great multinational corporations with little regard for national boundaries or sovereignty. The result was low investment at home (around half that of rivals) and diminishing productivity (Gamble 1985: 16). Market doctrines could not but welcome such footloose behaviour. Indeed, one of the very first acts of the Thatcher government was to encourage the tendency by completely abandoning exchange controls and the 1980s saw the British economy experiencing the Tragedy of the Commons (see pp. 41–2).

Whither the market?

It can be seen that the market fails to live up to the claims of its advocates on many counts. Although retaining an ability to orchestrate part of life, it cannot promote the common good without the state. Like fire, it is a good servant, but as a master it has the rationality of a volcano which must consume all it engulfs. The social democratic achievements of the post-war era saw the market reduced to servitude and it served well, producing material abundance without destroying the cohesion of society. Yet when it becomes master some individuals may benefit in the short term but ultimately the whole society will suffer. This has been at the core of the British problem.

The great ecological holocaust
The side-effects of individualistic self-seeking can range from minor irritants to the extremely serious. The idea of the Tragedy of the Commons argues that individual decisions must lead, with inexorable logic, to catastrophic consequences, including resource exhaustion and ecological havoc (see Hardin 1968). Environmental destruction is suffered by all, including entirely innocent generations yet unborn.

A firm pursuing profit will not be concerned with the side-effects of its operation if they do not show up on its balance sheets. Thus we have pollution of the rivers, depletion of the seas, poisoning of the atmosphere and grotesque architectural blots on the urban and rural landscape. One of the greatest problems of the post-war age is the process whereby a vast tonnage of metal grinds from one side of the country to the other at totally disproportionate cost, producing pollution, noise, endemic congestion and the blight of modern psychological life – stress. From the sub-atomic world to the macrocosm, scientists fight for ownership of our genes while governments fight to own the universe, promising a celestial Tragedy of the Commons (Laver 1986). All this results from people making market choices on the basis of what seems to be the optimal course for themselves. Moreover, rational companies pursue their trade in arms, rational countries stockpile them and the human species becomes a deadly virus upon the planet, a fateful terminal illness.

Peaceful uses of the market

Yet the fact that the unfettered market will not be best for the community does not mean that it can be abandoned altogether; it must play a vital role in a wide range of decisions within society. Hayek is correct to argue that the complexity of matching what people want with what will be produced can be effectively handled by the market. However, it cannot be left to itself. The genius of social democracy is to create a society in which the power of the market, like that of the atom, is harnessed to serve peaceful ends without leaving lethal contamination.

7 THE FALSE LOGIC OF COLLECTIVE ACTION

The US has been a hospitable climate for the doctrines of the individualists. Locke's hand guided the writing of the Constitution and Herbert Spencer, preaching his social Darwinist doctrines, was lionized in the establishment *salons*. This is the land where a man, with his horse and gun (the inalienable right to shoot the president), could live by his wits and his bravery. US legends celebrate great individualists – Wyatt Earp, Doc Halliday and Jesse James, the American dream is of the guy who makes it and the demonology tells of the feathered tribes, collectivist and warlike, their arrows sharp and their pagan totem poles mocking the true religion of the Protestant free market. It is not surprising that the prophets of the new denomination of the individualist religion, public choice theory, should hail from the new world.

The public choice theorists

For the most part the background of public choice theorists lies in the discipline of neo-classical economics. They have grown up in a world of simplicity where every person has a price; self-interest, rather than fundamental values, is the criterion of action. They advanced upon political science with a lean and hungry look, promising to be dangerous.

The Virginians
Public choice theorists apply the methodological individualistic reasoning of classical economics to the study of politics. In the van has been an intellectual task-force

hailing from the University of Rochester and Virginia Polytechnic and State University – the Virginia School. Prominent amongst the luminaries have been Downs, Buchanan, Tullock, Musgrave, Arrow, Lindblom, Black, Bamoul, Davis, Harsanyi, Olson and Niskanen (see Mitchell 1969). Thoughout their work is a strain which can be traced back to an earlier Virginian, Thomas Jefferson, one of the founding fathers of the US Constitution, who placed supreme confidence in the populist voice of individuals to curb government, and in the idea of individuals' freedom from the state, ideals enshrined in the term 'Jeffersonian Democracy'.

The intellectual pedigree

Public choice theory has long existed as an intellectual backwater, passing under various aliases: the mathematical approach to politics, rational choice theory, the theory of collective choice, the new political economy, the economic approach or even the economic theory of democracy. Although economics, the theory of games and probability theory provide its major sources, the work contains intimations of the individualistic positivism of Hobbes, the individual ethics of Locke and the utilitarian ideas of Bentham. It also derives much from the approach of logicians, physicists and mathematicians such as Borda, Condorcet, Laplace and the Reverend C. L. Dodgson, whose Wonderland, to which he despatched the precocious Alice, is scarcely less fantastical than the one constructed by the public choice theorists. In addition, the work owes much to a field termed (perhaps pretentiously) the 'strict study of politics' (Tullock 1965: 326–7), a title delivering an implicit rap on the knuckles for traditional political science. Today it is seen by some as a branch of political science although, as Tullock concedes, 'its true intellectual roots lie in other areas' (1965: 323). Indeed, writing in the genre displays an antipathy towards political scientists who, with their empirical and inductive approach to study, and their endorsement of collectivist decision-making, are presumably not given to strict study.

Although protesting that 'methodological individualism should not be confused with "individualism" as a norm for organising social activity' (Buchanan and Tullock 1962: vii), public choice theorists are ultimately ethical individualists. They espouse a full package of libertarian values including minimal government, individual freedom, atomistic populism and even, by implication, embrace the idea of a Lockean state of nature and a social contract.

The approach might have remained an academic freak-show, an intellectual Elephant Man, were it not for the fact that its extraordinarily right-wing conclusions and associated prescriptions attracted the attention of politicians seeking a rational basis for a militantly anti-social-democratic programme. Public choice theory left the fairground booth for the legitimate theatre, finding itself centre stage and bathed in the spotlight's heady glare. Needless to say, the effect was to unleash an upsurge of new talent keen to get in on the act. Covertly right-wing academics, including political scientists, emerged from the closet of the senior common room, proclaiming that they had long been speaking public-choice prose.

The proponents have not been shrinking academic violets; they are polemists as well as social scientists and the New Right think-tanks, such as the Institute of Economic Affairs, the Policy Studies Institute and the Adam Smith Institute were to be generous, if not lavish, in sponsoring their wit and wisdom. The individualism permeating British culture meant that the seeds were not to fall on stony ground. The anti-tax, anti-bureaucratic, anti-welfare state, anti-politics and ultimately anti-democratic message evoked strong resonances, not only in the masonic lodges and Women's Institutes of the home counties, but also in the bars, workingmen's clubs and launderettes of the cities.

Yet in applying a cold logico-deductive method to political life, public choice theory constitutes a hazardous voyage into uncharted intellectual waters for many of its midshipmen, and the result is some dangerous compass misreading and an extra-ordinary naivety about the real world of politics.

Methodological individualism and public choice

In public choice theory an individualist, market-type analogy is developed to explain political choices. Thus Buchanan and Tullock claim that the method 'incorporates political activity as a particular form of *exchange*; . . . as in the market relation' (1962: 19–20). This is not really politics at all. The concept of collective authority, as embodied in the idea of the state, is replaced by an image of a multiplicity of atomized individuals shaping public outcomes by accident rather than by design. Public choice theorists dispute the ontological status of corporate actors; the existence of political associations such as pressure groups, parties, corporations and, of course, the state itself, are nothing more than the existence of individuals. Yet para-doxically they do not dispute the existence of collectivities in the real world, since much ink and word-processor ribbon is expended discoursing upon their ill effects; they are cloaks for the self-interested behaviour of individuals – politicians and bureaucrats. A preoccupation with the individual suggests a favouring of democracy, but this is an unreal, mathematical populism, largely confined to the polling booth, with electoral systems conceived in terms of a political market-place.

The broad approach resembles the 'resolutive-compositive' method which Hobbes took from Galileo (see p. 9). Society is broken down into its smallest elements (individuals), axiomatic assumptions are made about their motivation (self-interest), and models are built by a Euclidian process of deduction. The empiri-cal world only enters as a final stage when 'predictions' deduced from the model are tested. In this latter stage lies their great claim to be more scientific (in the Popperian sense) than traditional political scientists. However, the process has a bogus, if not pretentious air, since they do not actually predict anything new (like the presence of a previously unknown planet or sub-atomic particle). Rather than the empirical test verifying the prediction, the prediction verifies the already known reality. For example, Downs's Proposition 2 proclaims biblically that 'both parties in a two party system agree on any issues that a majority of citizens strongly favour' (Downs 1957: 297) – an assertion of a well-attested finding of political science. The self-interest postulates seem merely to confirm in a myriad ways the basic principle that turkeys will not normally vote for an early Christmas.

Meeting public choice man: desert island risks

The axiomatic individual of the public choice theorist is much the same as the lonely, frightened figure inhabiting the Hobbesian natural landscape. He is a cousin of

Homo economicus, whose habitat is the uncomplicated world of the free market. Eschewing bonds of duty, comradeship, affection, honour or love, he does not have friends or fellows, only rivals and competitors. He is not a member of society and is unmoved by art, sympathy, creativity, altruism or love for anyone but himself. His behaviour is held to be rational in that he always calculates what is in his own interest before each act. With his simple, logically predictable behaviour he is, despite claims to the opposite (see Tullock 1965: 14), beyond reach of analysis in terms of true *Verstehen* – a seeing from within uniquely available to social scientists. Such people are held together only by the laws and contracts deemed necessary to make the market work. Through public choice theory the bleak and risky Robinson Crusoe existence of the market was to be extended to the whole of life.

Rational man and superman

The individual of public choice theory is even less real than *Homo economicus*. The latter (certainly in Hayek's view) is assailed by human doubt and intellectual limitation; it is the market that distils rationality from his behaviour. However, public choice man is a superman; his behaviour is held to be based upon perfect information and an absence of doubt. In this sense he is not a person but a bearer of roles, a mathematical creation to be placed in an equation.

Not only is he a superman, he is a bad man. We find a rephrasing of the doctrine of original sin which has long appealed to the right, a repeat of the overriding sentiment of Scottish philosopher David Hume (1711–71), that every man ought to be supposed a knave and to have no end other than private interest (Green and Grose 1882). However, while Hume believed the state could be constructed to control the knavery (largely through mixed government), public choice men are at their very worst when in political groups, parliaments, executives or state bureaucracies.

The hidden hand clenched

In addition to its view of the rational actor, public choice theory differs from that of the Austrian School in its ultimate prediction. The latter is optimistic, seeing the outcome of unplanned, egotistical market behaviour as a beauteous 'spontaneous order', dextrously moulded by the hidden hand. However, in the world of the public choice theorist the hidden hand clenches itself into an ugly fist. When the actors on this stage are given free reign the result is chaos and the Hobbesian nightmare approaches reality. Why is this? The answer lies in the context. Where the market, like a stern schoolmaster, brings out the very best in the human spirit, the institutions of politics have the edifying quality of Dickens's Fagin. For this reason the public choice theorists expend much of their energies in seeking to redesign the state, trying assiduously to remould the clay in the image of the market.

The public choice *Weltanschauung*

The naivety of the public choice world view may be likened to a primitive painting (Dunsire 1973: 127), a Lowry landscape peopled by matchstick people with matchstick cats and dogs. Tullock divides the terrain into 'the theory of committees and elections', the 'theory of parties and candidates' and the 'theory of constitutions' (Tullock 1965: 326–7). The following sections explore this landscape in terms of electoral behaviour, parties, pressure groups, bureaucracies and the local state.

Voters and elections: the constitutional bazaar

Since their universe is peopled by individuals rather than collectivities, it is hardly surprising that the public choice theorists devote a great deal of attention to voters and electoral systems. In fact, voting behaviour has always been a sitting duck for those who would apply mathematical techniques to the study of politics. The approach leads to naive 'consumer voting models' which conceive the state as a great supermarket where voters shop for policies as they would for washing powder. In this they are regarded as credulous morons, swearing allegiance to the party making the most extravagant promises (Himmelweit et al. 1985: 70). The result is a considerable amount of esoteric modelling, most of which dwells in a stratosphere of fantasy bearing little resemblance to the empirical theories of political science. In the real world, even though voters desire an increased standard of living, they do not naively expect the politicians to deliver it. Moreover, Alt discovered that the British people simply were not at all greedy or narrowly self-interested in economic matters (Alt 1979: 264). The consumer voting model is little more than an interesting fiction, the collective concept of class allegiance remaining by far the most consistent predictor of voting behaviour.

Auster and Silver (1979) visualize the state as a gigantic firm, although it is no workers' cooperative and the people it serves are not citizens but shareholders. They note that as private firms get larger so the owners' influence diminishes through widespread shareholding. This is seen as a deterioration (a process of entropy) which, revealingly, they liken to the growth of democracy. Shareholders have too small a stake to waste time in complaining about falling profits and slack management. By the same token, the voteholder in a democracy has no effective voice and is at the mercy of an Orwellian state.

Other public choice theorists are puzzled by the way the political market aggregates a whole range of different issues to be decided by so crude an instrument as a single election in which each elector has only a single vote. In one of the genre's classic studies, Kenneth Arrow (1951) expounded his 'impossibility theorem' to demonstrate that the wide range of individual preferences can never be aggregated into a single welfare function. However, political scientists know that nobody tries to do any such thing. Representative government is not expected to be government by referendum, and never could be.

Models have been devised by the public choice theorists to afford opportunity for ascertaining public opinions on this or that issue with greater subtlety. These include multiple votes, held like the money one spends in the market-place, to be divided amongst parties, candidates and policies. Again the nostrums would make a nonsense of the idea of representative government, the essential feature of democracy in the modern state. Taken to the extreme there would be no government, just a series of referendums, and the sum of the state would be no more than the sum of its parts.

Schumpeterian democracy

Although not sharing the right-wing ideology of the modern public choice theorists, it was Joseph Schumpeter who paved the way for an economic view of voting behaviour in his highly elitist model of party competition. This depicted modern democracy as an 'institutional arrangement for arriving at political decision in which individuals acquire the power to decide by means of a competitive struggle for the people's vote' (Schumpeter 1976: 269). This was obvious enough in Britain from the time of the great nineteenth-century Reform Act, but Schumpeter, an economist and sociologist, stressed the market analogy. This broad approach was commandeered by Downs, who postulated his *Economic Theory of Democracy* (1957), and was developed to an extraordinary degree of complexity by him and others. The intellectual contortions required of the voter extended well beyond the scope of most people, and even of some political scientists. To enter Downs's democracy one would need not a badge of citizenship, but a good degree in mathematics and symbolic logic. Fortunately for the British voter in a two-party system, the decision is merely a 'simple' subtraction between two 'expected utility incomes'!

$$E(U_{t+1}^A) - E(U_{t+1}^B) \text{ (Downs 1957: 39)}$$

Matters become more complicated with proportional representation and would call for postgraduate qualifications. In fact Downs and the mathematical wizards really lost sight of Schumpeter's essential point. He did not suppose complex calculating ability: 'the electoral mass is incapable of action other than a stampede' (Schumpeter 1976: 283). He argued that individuals do not expect to influence policy: 'we now take the view that the role of the people is to produce a government' (1976: 269). This is a view which has been easily accepted into modern political science, as was his stress on the advertising and sloganizing that were to become 'not accessories . . . [but] the essence of politics' (1976: 269).

The political agenda

There is a clear political agenda in the public choice prescriptions. Majority voting systems are distrusted because they are felt to encourage coalitions of minorities (log rolling) which ultimately threaten the hallowed rights of property through an unholy alliance of the have-nots. The Pareto optimality principle avers that no change is acceptable unless no one is made worse off – a fine recipe for the status quo. There is virtually no social advance possible which does not harm someone somewhere, even if it takes a mere pound from the pocket of an idle millionaire to restore the sight of a child.

Again, advocating greater use of referendums can generally be expected to produce 'No' answers on taxation questions, as did the celebrated Proposition 13 in the state of California. The referendum has the effect of atomizing the mass, of breaking the solidarity of party, group or class; we hear resounding echoes of the elitist fear of the 'tyranny of the majority' (Sugden 1981: 198).

Parties: the policy brokers

Parties, the mainsprings of modern politics, are seen by Downs as close analogues to firms in the free market, but maximizing votes rather than profits. This is placed above idology, which is mere Dayglo packaging to sell the produce and will be remodelled according to voters' tastes. In bipartisan systems parties will become almost indistinguishable, converging on the middle ground where the great mass of voters are believed to be – a situation which of course accords with the reality of consensus politics. Alternatively, a multi-party system will promote greater ideological differentiation, each party seeking a market niche. Generally the view is that party competition exerts an evil effect, leading to an escalation of promises to the masses and a growing tax burden for the affluent minority. Parties will employ devious strategies such as cobbling together a share of the vote by amalgamating various minorities with extravagant promises. Governing parties follow an electoral courtship cycle, enacting stern policies in the early years of power and seductive ones as nemesis approaches. Opposition parties will naturally try to outbid the government with even more generous promises and voters' expectations are progressively raised.

Things get even worse when governments try to escape the consequences of their profligacy by public borrowing, leading, *inter alia*, to growth in the money supply and inflation, which again tends to visit disproportionate pain upon the wealthy as the value of their investments falls. Moreover, government borrowing is said to 'crowd out' more productive private sector borrowing, reducing investment and retarding growth. This ties in with the free-marketeers' deep disapproval of Keynesianism.

Groups: the policy auction

The public choice theorists are not alone in noting the shortcomings of representative democracy. Pluralists agree, but argue that these are mitigated by a form of democratic life to be found beyond the ballot box in the interplay of pressure groups (Dahl 1956). However, the public choice theorists are deeply suspicious of such groups. Buchanan and Tullock declare: 'our conception of democratic process has much in common with that . . . which follows Arthur Bentley [1967] in trying to explain collective decision making in terms of the interplay of group interests', but 'at best, the analysis of group interests leaves us one stage removed from the ultimate choice making process which can only take place in individual minds' (Buchanan and Tullock 1962: 9). Generally the public choice theorists conclude that the pluralist process further escalates public expenditure.

Mancur Olson (1968) argues that rational individuals do not really wish to belong to pressure groups at all. They can obtain all the benefits (higher wages, shorter hours and so on) without incurring the cost of membership; that is, by free-loading. According to this analysis, membership is artificially induced through various forms of bribery (termed 'selective incentives') or the bullying of closed-shop agreements. Contrary to pluralist theory, the existence of groups is an artificial artefact of social life. Consequently, the demands they make are similarly unnatural and force public expenditure beyond its natural level.

Groups will form unholy alliances in the practice of log rolling, whereby certain of them will reach a secret agreement to support each other so that, in exchange for promoting a policy about which it is indifferent, a group will get support for its own cause. Not only does this increase the pressure on government for more expenditure, it distorts the democratic process since a third group, larger than the two log rollers, will be squeezed out.

Moreover, it is argued that rational groups will have no interest in making sacrifices for the general good (economic growth) when they can enjoy the collective benefit of successful policy without so doing – a form of collective free-riding (Olson 1982). A group will pursue only those interests which accrue uniquely to its own members. Unions will seek higher wages, cartels will push up prices, professional associations will restrict entry into their profession to increase their scarcity value, and so on. Once again public expenditure escalates.

The public choice theorists conclude that the groups which lose out most consistently in the pluralistic process are those opposing state spending, government borrowing and an increase in the money supply. They invariably shed a particular tear on behalf of the taxpayer. This anti-pluralist orientation was picked up with enthusiam by other New Right writers and politicians and much of their anti-group terminology ('overload', 'pluralist stagnation', 'the ungovernability of the state') entered the lexicon, to be encountered in academic papers, at party conferences and on the televised hustings.

These studies of parties and pressure groups share in common with pluralist theory a view of government as nothing more than a kind of referee, an auctioneer in a great bargaining process. Here policy outputs are explainable entirely in terms of the inputs: the demands of voters, parties and groups. However, other public choice theorists break open the black box to expose the inner workings of the machine.

Ministers and mandarins: inside the black box

The public choice theorists do not like what they find in the black box of the state: individuals whose only incursion into the free market is to negotiate the sale of their souls to the devil. Tullock cannot be accused of sitting on an academic fence: 'We are saddled with a large and inefficient bureaucracy' (1965: 221).

For the public choice theorists state administration is not the protection of citizens' rights or a quest for social justice but a labyrinthine world of public officialdom to be painted in garishly Machiavellian terms. Although Tullock does concede that 'bureaucrats are partly public interested' (1976: 27), there is no real place for a public service ethic. *Homo bureaucraticus* is an incorrigibly self-interested maximizer, not of profit (for such a concept does not exist in the public sector), but of the agency budget. He is preoccupied with the old game of empire building; if he advocates more education or health care of the masses it will not be out of fellowship or altruism, but for personal self-aggrandizement.

For William Niskanen (1971) there are two sets of actors in the process, corresponding to the suppliers and demanders in the market-place: officials and politicians. However, unlike participants in a real market, they are unconstrained by prudential considerations of cost and profit. Not only will the politicians promise the earth to get elected, the bureaucrats will eagerly give it to them. Niskanen's pinstriped maximizers seek the goals of high salary, generous perquisites, reputation, power, prestige, patronage and ease of job, and to secure them will connive, withhold information, lie and cheat in a manner that would make Sir Humphrey Appleby blush. The result is a dizzy, never-ending upwards spiral of 'oversupply' of goods and services in which the masses get far more education, health care, social services and so on than they could ever afford. Oversupply cannot be curbed by political assemblies because politicians, and the scrutiny committees they establish, far from being guardians of the public purse, walk in fear of being associated with spending cuts.

Stripped of its neologistic, scientific patina this is little more than the classic liberal critique of the threat of bureaucracy as put, *inter alia*, by Kafka, Orwell, and even Weber himself. However, an important difference is that public choice analysis implies that bureaucratic pathologies are necessarily entailed in the very idea of the organization, which is never anything other than the sum of its individual parts. In principle there is little or no scope for improvement in structural terms; state bureaucracies are mad, bad and exceedingly dangerous to know.

In the public choice scenario, state agencies not only resemble Frankenstein's monsters in their propensity to grow ever larger and destroy their creators, they are veritable Draculas cursed with immortality (Kaufman 1976). While unsuccessful firms are driven out of business by the stern logic of profitability, the grim reaper passes over the public sector. Once agencies are formed, officials, who owe their livelihoods to their continuance, use all their bureaucratic wiles to ensure survival well beyond their constitutional shelf life.

Not surprisingly, the New Right's answer is to drive a stake through the heart of these constitutional undead by rolling back the state frontiers. Alternatively, there could be a constitutional limitation of the state budget. Where this is not possible, competition must be introduced both between and within public agencies, even competition to provide the same service.

Public choice in the local state

Praise for local government might seem out of keeping with the general prescriptive thrust of the public choice theorists. The city, with its facility for bringing working people together in a threatening collectivity, has, since the industrial revolution, been a spectre to haunt the right.

Yet some public choice theorists see hope in the idea of local government. A system of municipalities provides a degree of decentralization resembling the market; they could compete against each other in a quest for efficiency. Charles Tiebout (1956) argued that, if local authorities were sufficiently small, people would shop around for the best place to live, voting not with their hands but with their feet. This would reduce local taxes as authorities vied with each other for the nomadic citizenry exercising Hirschman's opportunities of exit, voice or loyalty (1970).

However, this is no plea for genuine local government; democracy is entirely eclipsed by the market. Those without the resources to exit are obliged to remain, yet the voice option is denied them as the vote is devalued. The rational authority cannot provide the social services they need for fear of driving away those who would fund them. Britain's decaying inner cities testify to a grim element of truth in Tiebout's thesis.

Public choice management

The public-choice-inspired reforms (hiving off, contracting out, compulsory competitive tendering, deregulation, privatization, internal marketization and, most important of all, managerialism) introduced in both central and local government were in essence nothing more than a return to some very old management precepts which had developed during the Fordist era of inflexible mass production for mass markets. Broadly this is Taylorism, and it means deskilling the workforce, lowering morale and treating people as machines with no greater commitment to the work than the size of the pay-packet. Not only is such a model politically degrading in the social democratic state, by the standards of the Japanese, the pace-setters in modern management, it is entirely outmoded. Today the world has entered a post-Fordist era where flexibility, high motivation, commitment and 'flat' (rather than hierarchical) management styles predominate. Quality of work cannot be imposed from without as is implied in the hiving-off solution; top-down (bossy) management styles destroy public sector morale and the idea of the contract introduces a rigidity entirely at odds with the post-Fordist era and in stark contrast to the 'mutual understanding' which Japanese management practices seek to develop (Murray 1991).

The return to nature

Public choice theorists share with Locke and the neo-classical economists a fear and loathing of the state. Their prescriptions may be crystallized as a call for the minimal state and the idea of the natural freedom of individuals to do their own thing. 'Christian idealism . . . must be tempered by an acceptance of the moral imperative of individualism'; 'Love thy neighbour, but also let him alone' is recommended as 'the overriding ethical precept for Western liberal society' (Buchanan and Tullock 1962: 303). However, their justifications for the minimalist state are essentially utilitarian – life will be better without the bureaucrats. This opens their case to direct empirical refutation: has life really been worse in the era of 'big government'? We address this sixty-four-thousand-dollar question in Chapter 9.

However, for further protection the New Right can turn to US philosopher Robert Nozick. While not of the Austrian School or a public choice theorist, his extreme libertarianism makes him welcome for at least an embrace in the bed of either.

At the outer reaches of the state

Nozick seeks to breathe new life into the natural rights thinking of Locke. His main statement is in *Anarchy, State and Utopia* (Nozick 1974). Only individuals are real and their rights are bestowed by nature, justified on deontological grounds; whether or not their preservation maximizes happiness is irrelevant. Natural rights are moral absolutes; their violation by the state is always wrong and cannot be justified on utilitarian grounds. Hence the minimal state is itself a moral necessity.

Nozick imagines a state of nature which he designates his 'rest position'; here there are absolute rights to the 'natural' individual freedoms. A person has an inviolable right to his or her own body and to the produce (property) generated by any labour that body might undertake, subject only to the constraint that this does not restrict the same rights in others. Nozick denies the idea of positive rights (to welfare, health, education and so on), arguing that the individual must not be treated as a means to some utilitarian end; people should not be made worse off in order to improve the position of others. His call is for a most extreme version of the minimalist state, its essential role being the policing of the fundamental rights and enforcing contracts between individuals. It should not tax, confiscate property, undertake public works or help the underprivileged.

His elevation of individual freedom from the state as the pre-eminent human right leads to a defence of profound inequality, not only in the ownership of property but in all areas of social justice, including health care. It is not that existing inequalities are good in themselves, but their removal would entail the violation of more fundamental and important rights. We hear echoes of public choice electoral theories when Nozick argues that natural rights can only be removed by the state under the consent, not of a majority, but unanimously; this is the cold kiss of death to any idea of a redistributive state.

The sneaking-up state

For Nozick the state is a kind of monopolistic protection and punishment agency, forcing its clients to pay for its services through the tax system (Nozick 1974: 108). Strictly speaking it should not exist; the danger of infringing rights makes it impossible to move from the anarchy of nature to even a minimal state. Under similar circumstances the Hobbesian and Lockean people consent to a contractual mutual limitation on freedom in their long-term (utilitarian) interests. However, Nozick finds this unnecessary, arguing that a process of economic exchange (the market) will appear naturally and cause a minimal state to sneak up without conscious design – another manifestation of the hidden hand. In this way no one can be held guilty of the infringements on liberty.

Such an argument rules out any possibility of an Aristotelian discussion on the nature of the state. However, we shall argue in Chapter 8 that the sneaking-up state is an historical fantasy, no more likely than the signing of contracts.

Beyond the frontier: justice at high noon

Journeying beyond the borders of Nozick's libertarian state one comes to the land of the anarchists, or anarcho-capitalists. Murray Rothbard (1978) and David Friedman (1973) ('Son of Milton') depict a true US fantasy-land where a man and his gun are alone against the world. This re-creation of the legendary Wild West would remove the state altogether; from policing, from the army and even from the law courts. There would not even be a sheriff to round up a posse.

From prediction to predilection: 'What to do? What to do?'

It is clear that, in their readiness to slide from description and prediction to prescription and rhetoric, the public choice theorists belie their self-proclaimed status as practitioners of a positive science. Despite Hayek's warning against the practice, the literature is replete with constitutional engineering, ranging from tips of the 'inside dopester' variety to elaborate blueprints for complex electoral systems to be employed at various stages of the political process. Tullock unashamedly concludes his study of bureaucracy with a chapter entitled 'What to do? What to do?' (1965: 221). In their reforming mission to repair a world which has for so long laboured under the Aristotelian delusion that man was a political animal, the allegedly fictional postulates become empirical truths and *Verstehen* insights. Tullock reapplies Hobbes's psychological method (see p. 9), claiming that 'we understand how others feel or act because we know how we would act or feel under similar circumstances' (1965: 14), and emerges with similarly uncharitable results.

Strange harmony of contrasts

While they may not entirely favour the constitutional engineering of Lee Harvey Oswald, the project of the public choice theorists is to limit the state by curtailing the activities of bureaucrats, elected representatives, pressure groups and ultimately the electorate, with its irritating tendency to vote for more than it can afford. There seems to be a paradox here: while bureaucratic egoism leads public choice theorists to call for less state action, that of entrepreneurs leads them to call for more market activity. Yet it is not really a paradox. The two desiderata harmonize in warm symbiosis to repeat the neo-Squealer dictum, 'market good, state bad': more consumer sovereignty, less political sovereignty.

For Hayek the problem of state activity lies largely in the economic field, arising from the sheer impossibility of gaining the kind of synoptic view required for state planning and control. Moreover, in trying to do so government will become totalitarian and the people are on the slippery *Road to Serfdom*. To this public choice theorists add that the state is not really an entity at all, merely a collection of self-seeking individuals who will subvert the process of government for their own purposes. Hence both regiments of the New Right join hands and sing, not the same tune, but with the close harmony of a barbershop duo.

Public choice theory as political science

The public choice theorists express puzzlement that their methods have not been used more in political science. There are few grounds for such surprise. In the first place, the study of politics draws upon a richer and deeper intellectual vein than the limited vision afforded by methodological individualism. More importantly, the individualism of liberal economists and public choice theorists cannot furnish a basis for an approach to real world politics. Industrial corporations, multinational conglomerates, international associations, wars, unions, parties, municipalities, families, personalities and so on have no place on this simplistic model railway layout. The thin cardboard cut-out who replaces Aristotle's sublime political man removes all subtlety from the understanding of complex human behaviour. Central concepts, such as political culture, class and power, which lie at the heart of political science, largely disappear from view (Therborn 1982: 226). Rather than political science this is intellectual reductionism by the discipline of economics. It entirely fails to understand some of the essential features of the study of politics which, by definition, is about collectivist action and the processes of compromise and conciliation (Crick 1964).

Buchanan, and his colleague Tullock, are themselves economists. He confesses that it would be 'presumption in the extreme for us to claim . . . that we have mastered even the accepted "classics" [sic] of political philosophy sufficiently to measure our own preliminary investigation and analysis against some wider criteria than our own subjective standards' (Buchanan 1962: 307). While commendably modest, this is an unusual basis for scholarship. Most people who have not mastered the classics of nuclear physics refrain from lengthy discourses on the subject. Yet economists are not distinguished by self-doubt. Thus born-again New Rightist John Vaizey explains that the 'failure' of Richard Titmuss, one of the intellectual fathers of the British welfare state, was in part 'because the economists were cleverer and had many more tricks up their sleeves' (1983: 78)

It is by no means without significance that most public choice theory comes from the US where the tradition of the neutral bureaucrat is not so well entrenched and the spoils system is still very much in evidence. Even so, this hardly justifies the view of the public service as something little better than the Mafia, presided over by elected godfathers making the scroungers of society offers they cannot refuse, and taking from the violin case of consensus politics the machine gun of taxation.

Notwithstanding the romanticized Lone Ranger folklore of the US, the Red Indians, collectivist and kindly, welcomed the individualistic, pale-faced conquistadors. It was the acquisitive ideology of the latter which obliged Custer to make his last stand. In modern society Prisoners' Dilemma scenarios proliferate and only the state can secure the common good.

8 REASSERTING THE COMMUNAL ETHIC

In previous chapters it has been argued that the atomized life, where each pursues his or her self-interest, does not produce the best for anyone in the long run. Smith's hidden hand, Hayek's spontaneous order and the trickle-down effect are great illusions effected with mirrors and false-bottomed boxes by moustachioed music-hall conjurors. However, the objections do not end with this essentially utilitarian critique. In this chapter we go on to argue that the sense of community gains its highest justification not as a means to an end, but as an end in itself, an indispensable component of the good life which we all seek.

The heart of the community

In addition to the luxury which castaways may choose for themselves, the BBC offers two standard gifts to those it admits to the establishment pantheon, *Desert Island Discs*. However, of the Bible and Shakespeare, the former is largely redundant baggage. In this fantasy paradise for the individualist there is no neighbour to love, no enemy to whom may be proffered the other cheek, and no trespasser to forgive. Even after over a decade of Thatcherism, most of the BBC's castaways vow to build rafts and escape, the instinct for community remaining within each human soul.

A spirit of community is natural to the human condition. At its most elemental it lies in the idea of the family, the imagery of which suffuses Christian ethics; people are brothers and sisters and God is the Father. We are enjoined, not to barter with our neighbours, but to love them; if we sell our old car we must do unto the prospective purchasers as we would have them do unto us – not a maxim for a successful market engagement. Hence it is not surprising that, throughout the 1980s and into the 1990s, some of the most trenchant criticisms of the New Right came from the Christian Church. There was talk of the 'Pharisee society' and policies (and, by clear implication, policy-makers) were characterized as 'wicked'.

It is one of life's beguiling curiosities that, while the right piously preaches the virtues of the family (nuclear, extended and Royal), there is no thought of extending its principles to society. Yet the state as family is more than an analogue; from early times it formed the basis for a social organization which ensured nothing less than the survival of the species.

The natural market or the instinctive community?

The idea of an instinct towards a communal, mutually supportive life stands in direct contradiction to the state of nature envisioned by New Right liberals, where the community, as a body with rules and ties, is a mere artefact created by contract to permit the operation of a more natural association – the market. For Adam Smith the instinct to barter was embedded deep within human nature (Smith 1976: 17) and, in similar vein, Nozick (1974) argues that market activities come first, leading the state to sneak up on people, without even the need for a notional contract. Always, the joy of a good bargain comes before the instinct to fellowship. The state is an affront to nature, intervention in the market being as misguided as Canute's attempt to confound the laws of time and tide.

Yet there is no empirical evidence that the propensity to live together is less natural than the great instinct which draws men and women, like migratory birds under the compulsion of the earth's magnetic field, to Sotheby's or Fortnum and Mason's. Patterns of exchange have in all probability existed from earliest times, but cannot logically predate the community (Lindblom 1977). 'Hobbes was wrong' says. Lucy Mair; although intrepid, panama-hatted, western explorers were blind to the sophistication of the cultures they disrupted, 'every primitive society recognizes in some way that fellow citizens have mutual obligations' (Mair 1962: 35).

In the natural history of *Homo sapiens* on Planet Earth, political theory is but a recent invention; before its appearance people had lived together, their actions guided by a mysterious subconscious as well as the reasoning mind. Various capacities ensured the survival of the species during the millennia of its prehistory, although the physical strength of so puny an animal would hardly be one of them; nor would an ability to strike a sharp deal in the Portobello Road or speedily unload a shaky portfolio before a City crash.

Our wode-daubed forebears of the Upper Palaeolithic became the dominant human type because they were socially solid with an intense sense of community. Living in bands or hordes they were able to defend themselves and develop life-sustaining hunting and agricultural practices (the mode of production). These people were not looking to sign a Lockean contract to relinquish a treasured natural freedom. Indeed, nature was a many-headed hydra and they were engaged in a life-or-death struggle against her thousand natural shocks. In this environment, *Homo economicus*, engaged in the lunatic war of all against all, would have left scant record in the history texts of the dolphins or apes who would have inherited the earth.

The life-preserving instinct came, not out of rational calculation but, like sexual appetite, by serendipity, and modern people inherit these atavistic drives. Just as sex continues to provide a pleasurable diversion (even for *Homo economicus* when the stock exchange closes), so our communal instinct remains part of our primeval inheritance. The desire for community is not rational but instinctive; fellowship is a sublimely good feeling, better than making money. Selfish people, like Ebenezer Scrooge, are rarely popular or happy; loneliness is seen as one of the curses of modern fragmented society and solitary confinement remains a terrible form of psychological torture.

The state and the good life

When the ancient Greeks contemplated the nature of the good life it was in the sense of community that they found it. The state was seen as the highest form of community and they did not agonize about a rational reason for recognizing an obligation to it. Hobbes's great question would have seemed as absurd as seeking an intellectual justification for a young man's fancy in spring. Plato himself asks: 'Does not the worst evil for a state arise from anything that tends to render it asunder and destroy its unity, while nothing does it more good than whatever tends to bind it together and make it one?' (Cornford 1941: 159). In his clarion funeral oration, Pericles celebrated the Athenian ideal, declaring: 'We do not say that a man who takes no interest in politics is a man who minds his own business; we say he has no business here at all' (Thucydides 1954: 118–19). However, the Greek view of citizenship was not truly communal since women, slaves and the lower orders were excluded. The Christian ideal of universal brotherhood and sisterhood was to extend the concept to embrace all, from the high and mighty to the most lowly.

The classical period of western history passed through the great era of the Roman Empire which ended with its fall in the fifth century AD. It was succeeded by the medieval period and the Dark Ages, when religious dogma determined the way people lived. This was terminated in the Renaissance of the fifteenth century which, with its rediscovery of ancient learning, marked the birth of the modern period, precipitating the Reformation which shattered the traditional authority in religion. Close upon the heels of these great events came the rise of positive science in the seventeenth century, which was to change the basis of knowledge and elevate the power of reason, leading to the eighteenth-century Enlightenment. Although political thought cast off the strait-jacket of tradition-based political authority, the ideas of community were not extinguished. It is from the modern period that we take up the story.

The enlightened community

The Enlightenment thinkers believed in the power of positive science to discover nature's laws and saw social life as something malleable and capable of infinite improvement. From Voltaire and Diderot came a vision of nature mastered and the great French *Encyclopédie* was the new bible.

The English individualists, with their cold and calculating view of life, promised to be frigid bedfellows and, as such, had greatly appealed to the sensibilities of their countrymen. Yet in the warmer climes of Europe, where people were unembarrassed by the embrace or the kiss, there developed philosophies which added fraternity and equality to liberty. Contemplation of these was to lead to the most momentous upheaval in modern politics: the French Revolution. The movement owed much to one who refused to ally with the *encyclopédistes* and their deification of pure reason: a wild, contradictory, Swiss-born bohemian – Jean-Jacques Rousseau.

Rousseau: the social contract

Rousseau (1712–78) was an individualist of sorts, with a passion for freedom. Like Hobbes and Locke he imagined a state of nature, but placed a quite different construction on the meaning and implications of liberty. The first chapter of his great work, *The Social Contract* (1762), opens with the ringing declaration that 'Man is born free; and everywhere he is in chains' (Rousseau 1913: 3). He saw the alleged natural freedom to pursue selfish ends as bondage to the appetites and slavery to the passions, while submission to a Hobbesian Leviathan 'is to suppose a people of madmen' (Rousseau 1913: 7).

Rousseau's state of nature was no Hobbesian inferno and his people were not selfish egoists; they were 'noble savages' moved by conscience and altruism as well as self-interest. When they were bad, they were made so by bad society. The state should bring out the best in them by reflecting what he termed the *volenté générale* (general will), something greater than a utilitarian accountant's balance sheet reflecting the 'passions of petty self-interest'.

True freedom can only be realized through the communal life in which individuals voluntarily act for the good of all and, in so doing, develop finer qualities of justice, conscience and morality. What if an individual is unwilling to act altruistically? Here Rousseau controversially proclaims that the state will *force* a person to be free. Essentially he is concerned to rid people of 'self-love'. Only through the state can this higher moral plane be attained; other associations (classes, parties, pressure groups) would merely reflect sectional interest. In *Emile*, he writes that the state institutions 'are those best able to denature man, to take away his absolute existence and to give him a relative one, and to carry the *moi* into the common unity' (quoted in Vaughan 1962: 145). The will is not to be crushed; it is to be generalized so that self-interest is seen in terms of communal good.

How does the individual know what is best for the community? Philosophers from Aristotle to J. S. Mill have believed such knowledge to be reserved to a virtuous elite, but Rousseau saw no complication. Although he argued in *Emile* that education should lead the people to conflate self-interest with the general will, wisdom was really a matter of instinct: we know what is right from within the heart, and our truest instincts are fraternal.

Essentially he calls for a form of democracy penetrating deeper than the right to vote – a full participation by all citizens in communal life. To this end he favoured the Greek notion of the small city-state. Equality is necessary for Rousseau because the individual is fully realized only when liberated from those things which exclude honest and simple sociability, such as poverty and excessive wealth. Yet the fact that people do not seek to triumph over others does not suppress individuality. Quite the reverse, sociability will value uniqueness. In his *Confessions* Rousseau avows: 'I am

not made like any of those I have seen. If I am not better, at least I am different'
(quoted in Crick 1987: 13). The true communitarian will foster and treasure the
uniqueness of each individual.

It is difficult to underestimate Rousseau's influence over thought and events.
He was the father of the great romantic movement in the arts and in life, influencing European literature, inspiring modern child-centred education and of
course making a profound impact on political thought. In the latter he replaced
atomized theories with a great organic view of the state which inspired the moral
philosophy of Kant and Hegel's philosophy of right and led to German and English
idealism which was to lay the foundations of the modern social democratic state. In
the world of events he will be honoured uniquely as the inspiration for the French
Revolution, the momentous social upheaval which opened up new vistas for
mankind.

Kant: the kingdom of ends

The widely influential moral philosopher Immanuel Kant (1724–1804) lived
largely apart from the upheavals of the age and was the deepest of the Enlightenment thinkers. Accepting Protestant ethics, he was, like Rousseau, sceptical of
reason, which he believed had a compulsion to reach empty and irrational conclusions. Although a liberal, he argued that individual autonomy was to be expressed
not in satisfying the appetites, nor even in pursuit of some greater utilitarian
good, including the pursuit of personal salvation, but in observing self-legislated
moral principles (maxims), the essence of which was treating others as ends rather
than as means. First and foremost was the 'categorical imperative', a canon of
absolutely right behaviour regardless of circumstances of time and place: 'Act so
that the maxim of your action can be willed as a universal law' (Kant 1948: 76).
Morality must follow a sense of duty derived from the idea of the communal (or
universal) good. His law of reason was, like Rousseau's social contract, a basis for
realizing a sense of fulfilment deeper than prudential self-interest. The framework
in which this sense of duty can be fostered is an ideal community, a 'kingdom of
ends'. Initially he saw the French Revolution as moving towards this ideal state, but
later withdrew his support in the belief that imperfect mortals could never make such
an approach.

The French Revolution: the best of times, the worst of times

In the history of the modern political community the French Revolution stands as an
indelible landmark. After its dramatic career the nation could be seen as a basis for
the spirit of community, a focus for political processes and an object of loyalty
(Gamble 1981: 132–6). Rousseau's vision was presented to a society which mocked
his communal ideals of liberty, equality and fraternity. The individual was defined
as a subject of the monarch, Louis XVI, and by inclusion in one of the three great
estates of the realm: the clergy, the nobility and the bourgeoisie. It was a corrupt
edifice of privilege and hearts and minds were ready to respond to the emotion and
reason in his compelling message.

Initially the revolution was led by liberals with individualistic sentiments similar
to those which inspired the American revolutionaries and the English Whigs. They

attacked royal absolutism and ancient privilege and the 1789 Declaration of the Rights of Man established that people were not subjects but citizens, entitled to equal natural rights. The Constitution of 1791 enfranchised a large section of the male population, established elected local governments and judges, opened up a host of state positions to all, honoured the rule of law, and even applied progressive taxation. A democratic spirit permeated the cultural air; political clubs blossomed (the largest being the Jacobins) and popular debate was extended through newspapers and pamphleteering.

Yet in a population of some 26 million there could be little of the participatory ideals of Rousseau; property qualifications restricted parliamentary candidature and a distinction was made between passive, non-voting citizens (servants and the very poor) and others. The revolutionary train could hardly be expected to halt at such a point. The ideal of liberty (as freedom from the autocratic state) was seen as only part of the project; the egalitarian ideal demanded a state that would intervene in the interests of the poor against the propertied so that liberty could be enjoyed by all. Events moved on, government fell under the radical wing of the Jacobins and the monarchy was replaced by the Republic.

A new constitution made the country more democratic than any in the world, greatly alarming other European elites, including that of Britain, which determined to destroy the new regime and restore the monarchy. Dramatic events led the Jacobins to launch the Terror against their internal opponents and unleashed a new and awesome power in the spirit of citizenship. Many volunteered for surveillance committees, to serve in the citizens' National Guard and, when war broke out in 1792, to fight in the army which successfully withstood the great professional battalions of Europe. The new republic proved uniquely able to mobilize its people in an almost total commitment to the state community.

Although Robespierre and the Jacobins were overthrown in 1794 and the military dictatorship of Napoleon imposed, momentous changes had been wrought. The *Code Napoleon* accepted the principle in the Declaration of the Rights of Man that sovereignty rested not with the monarch but the nation. Nationalism could generate a potent and meaningful sense of community and hence could effectively promote liberty, fraternity and equality.

Despite its failure, the revolution remained central to the spirit of modernity. The democratic overthrow of traditional structures of authority was seen as a necessary condition for the unfolding of enlightened ideas. All ideologies, whether socialist or liberal, were united in recognizing this. The statesmen of the old empires recoiled in alarm with good reason; democracy was welded inseparably to an electric power of nationalism.

The conservative reaction: fear of democracy
However, the forces of nationalism, once unleashed, were not only to be harnessed by the forces of revolution. There arose a conservative reaction, paradoxically evoking the idea of the national community as a basis for resisting change. In England Edmund Burke (1729–97) fashioned an elaborate anti-revolutionary philosophy. The idea that rights and laws could be established on the basis of reason was seen as an irreverent disregard for the wisdom of the ages. Radical change was against nature; communities and states were not of human design but were products of

organic evolution, each uniquely fitted to its place and time. This sense of community extended beyond the present to embrace generations past and yet unborn, and the former should be cherished and passed on to the latter.

Yet Burke spoke with a forked tongue. The repudiation of the rationalist tradition as it had developed through Hobbes, Descartes, Locke, Leibniz and Bentham was limited and opportunistic. It was fear of the French Revolution and of democracy which inspired his pen. His fidelity to the spirit of community did not extend to the economic sphere, where he venerated the doctrines of Adam Smith. Hence, although a Whig, his calculatedly unsystematic thought provided a *raison d'être* for the modern Conservative Party, combining freedom for the market with ancient patterns of elitism, deference and stern discipline for the masses.

Burke's condemnation of the French Revolution was countered by another great voice for the communal spirit, the radical English outlaw Thomas Paine (1737–1809), who had participated in the French Revolution when he became an elected representative, only to be imprisoned during the Terror. His revolutionary tract, *The Rights of Man* (1791), which was banned as seditious in England, accepted the universal natural rights of Locke but argued that these did not imply a civil society sealed off from the attentions of government. A life in which some individuals pursued their own advantage against the interest of the mass was seen as entirely the opposite of what nature might be said to have intended. In *The Rights of Man* he wrote: 'Man did not enter into society to become *worse* than he was before, nor to have fewer rights than he had before, but to have those rights better secured' (quoted in Eccleshall 1986: 110). In his espousal of popular sovereignty, and the rights of all rather than those of an elite, Paine radicalized the liberalism of Locke and exposed the political agenda of many who preached in the cause of freedom.

Making democracy safe

Some who accepted the individualist creed felt, nevertheless, that a new sense of community was required which would mitigate its impoverishing social effects while containing the disruptive forces of radicalism. French thinker Alexis de Tocqueville (1805–59) believed that democracy could be made good or bad by human design. He wrote of a need to lift men's minds above egoism and make them 'aware at every moment that they belong each and all to a vaster eternity' (Tocqueville 1971: xiv). He influenced the English utilitarian J. S. Mill, in whom we are able to appreciate how the crude individualism of the seventeenth-century thinkers could be developed in a manner which did not violate communal values. Although a liberal, Mill did not defend freedom on the grounds of pre-social rights. He argued that if people's interests are regarded as fixed pre-socially, with society nothing more than a means to secure them, then it is impossible to derive other liberal freedoms such as those of conscience, assembly, religion, speech and so on, which have no meaning outside society. Indeed, this category of freedoms is actually denied by the allegedly natural freedom of ownership (see p. 67)

While accepting it, Mill did not glorify egoism, seeing Bentham as concerned with crudely materialistic values. The good life required the individual to consider the desires, and enjoy the affections, of others, and a 'greater morality' which 'depends essentially upon considerations which Bentham never so much as took into account' (quoted in Kymlicka 1991: 16). His view of individualism was wider and more complex than that of the earlier utilitarians; freedom should realize the potential of each person in all respects, not merely the economic. Paradoxically, he employed the principles which justified the market to support humane values which would undermine it. Indeed, his *Principles of Political Economy* (1848) was a rethinking of Smith's *Wealth of Nations* in which he defended trade unions as a means of enabling workers to bargain with firms on a fair basis.

Mill's wide-ranging social prescriptions imply the kind of permissive society abhorred by the practical people of the Thatcherite tendency. His development of liberal thought exposes the political motivation behind the project of the New Right. Liberalism as developed by him and others, such as Rawls, has no place for the narrow selfishness seen as central to Thatcherism. Yet Mill remained a man of his time, a time of elitism. With de Tocqueville he feared full democracy. The unruly hordes could only mean trouble, and it was in his essay *On Liberty* (1859) that he used the phrase to give his bourgeois fellows sleepless nights: 'the tyranny of the majority'. Equality in the franchise should be withheld until the populace was fully trained in civic virtue, although this could come through the educative effect of political participation. The management of the municipalities (through election to local councils) and the workplace (through worker participation) both offered opportunities for the development of a sense of community.

However, a full sense of community is more than a means of containing the mass, it is an integral part of the good life. Another pattern of thought set in motion by Rousseau saw the community in more positive terms.

The state as organism

Rousseau showed how to speak of the liberal ideas of rights, the state of nature and the contract without anti-communitarian conclusions. He made it possible to see the state as an organism. In the eighteenth century certain 'biological' political theorists went to extraordinary lengths to describe the state in organic terms. Although some of their flights of fancy were absurd (they decided the state was masculine), the essential idea that all members of the state form a single entity offered a potent image. An organism could not exist if its organs engaged in a war of all against all. The good of each part is inextricably bound up with the good of the whole; a person with a diseased lung is incapacitated as a whole person.

This holistic perspective has profound implications for study. It underlies the functionalist approach pioneered by anthropologists like Radcliffe Brown (1881–1955) and Malinowski (1884–1942), in which social processes are meaningful only in terms of the whole community, and was adapted for the study of industrial societies by sociologists like Talcott Parsons and Robert Merton. It is also entailed in the systems thinking developed by biologist Ludwig von Bertalanffy (1956), which stresses the interrelatedness of all phenomena. Systems theory was imported into political science by David Easton, who argued that 'the phenomena of politics tend to cohere and to be mutually related' (Easton 1953: 97). Today the logic of holism is to be found in that most modern of worlds, cybernetics, the essence of which is communication between mutually related parts (Deutsch 1964; Hodgson 1984: 46).

In the holistic view the energy of the whole is greater than the sum of its parts, through the generation of *synergy*. Hence, 15 men working together according to a plan will be better at scoring tries than 15 random individuals fighting each other on a field; if there is such a thing as a team then there is such a thing as society.

Hegel: the divine idea

The organic view of the state was elaborated by one of the most influential thinkers of the modern age, Georg Hegel (1770–1831), a German philosopher who spent his youth in the heady days of the French Revolution, first intoxicated by the events, but living to experience a sour aftertaste.

Although a liberal, Hegel has given one of the most influential and extreme expositions of the communal nature of human life. He argued that the idea of the individual in a state of nature was illusory; human nature was itself a product of social interaction. Hence the meaning of rights could only be discussed in the light of real world social arrangements, particularly the family, civil society and the state. In *The Philosophy of Right* (1821) he portrayed individuals as both self-interested and altruistic (Hegel 1942). Altruism characterized behaviour within the family, where affection, benevolence and loyalty were predominant; it was the sphere of 'particular altruism'. In contrast, civil society was moved by self-interest, with the market determining who got what; it brought all members of the community into interaction as the sphere of 'universal egoism', the antithesis of the family. The third association is the synthesis of the first two: the thesis and anti-thesis. This was the state, the highest ethical ideal, the divine idea. Relationships within the state resembled those within the family but had the universality of the market, a sphere of 'universal altruism', binding all citizens in an organic whole. Only in the service of the state is the individual truly free: 'All the worth which the human being possesses . . . he possesses only through the state' (Kohn 1955: 110–11).

Hegel's model subsumes both Lockean civil society and the communal state of Rousseau. He does not deny the market or private property, but argues for an ethically superior level of existence. Self-interest is acknowledged, but not seen as the most elevated basis for behaviour, and may conflict with the ethical demands of the state. Thus, since property is accepted as a basis for genuine membership of civil society, it cannot follow that some should be without; they could not be full citizens, their loyalty would be in doubt and the state would be weakened.

The organic state in easy steps

In late-nineteenth-century England a group of influential thinkers were able to promote the ideas of Hegel. They formed the school of English Idealists and their most notable member was Thomas Hill Green (1836–82), an Oxford scholar reared on the classics and influenced by Aristotle. He modified Hegel's view of the state for home consumption, leavening collectivism with a form of radical individualism. He sought to draw from the idea of the individual an argument for community and citizenship, which he believed to lie latent as an instinct. For Green the state was not all-consuming (many crimes had been committed in the name of 'national honour'), its interest could not be seen as an ethical end in itself, and the individual could be justified in disobeying. Yet he agreed that its purpose was a 'common good' distinct from the sum of individually achieved happiness. In securing the common good the state makes the dramatic move from the negative role of protecting freedom to the positive one of promoting it through social welfare. A cohesive, organic community is only possible where all have the material means to participate. The capitalist system does not ensure this, so the state must intervene; the maxims of Ricardo and Malthus must be modified by the claims of social cohesion. Green was criticized by Berlin (1970) for laying the foundations of an oppressive society; the society which positively confers freedom can also erode it. However, Green was not seeking to make society oppressive in the name of freedom, rather to 'enable' freedom by removing obstacles and offering favourable conditions. His society would neither force people to be free nor force them to self-realization; self-effort is always required (Simhony 1991).

Thus the English Idealists were feeling towards a central tenet of the social democratic platform and their influence was by no means indirect. Lloyd George and Winston Churchill, active in the great liberal social reforms of the early twentieth century, heeded their words and William Beveridge left the cloisters of Oxford, where Green's influence was pervasive, to draw the blueprint of the post-war welfare state.

However, in addition to this organic thinking, there is another great part to be written into the communal score: socialism, an insistent ideological drumbeat marking the rhythm of the twentieth century.

Socialism and community

Socialism goes beyond the call for democracy articulated by constitutional radicals, who thought that full participation in the life of the polity would ensure social justice, to attack not only the individualist ethic but also the material basis of society. The idea of community has been central to most socialist thinking; William Morris (1834–96), founder of the Socialist League, believed fellowship to be heaven itself and its absence the very definition of hell.

The release of socialism from its original association with sandal-wearing well-meaning eccentrics to become the major ideological challenge to liberalism came through its practical linking with the rise of the industrial working class (Gamble 1981: 104). The potential power of mass action demonstrated in the French Revolution showed that socialism could become a doctrine of class war in pursuit of human welfare.

In search of Utopia

An early socialist thinker was French aristocrat, Claude Saint-Simon (1760–1825), who was inspired by the French Revolution. His ideas were spread by his one-time secretary, the sociologist Auguste Comte (1798–1857). Little concerned with democracy, he envisioned a centrally planned industrialized economy administered for the common good, a vision to find its extreme manifestation in communism. Another French socialist was François Fourier (1772–1837), born into a bourgeois family impoverished by the revolution. He viewed large-scale industrialization not as progress but as impoverishment; work should not merely be useful but spiritually fulfilling. Unable to exalt with Smith in the joys of the pin factory, he found the division of labour a diabolical insult to human creativity. Like Rousseau he saw true virtue in the simple, unsophisticated individual, favouring the industry of small craftsman and farmers, working and living in cooperatives of fewer than 2,000 (*phalanstères*). Yet his prescriptions were fantastical in the light of the industrial imperatives of the age; some experimental communes were established but were short lived.

A third key figure was Pierre-Joseph Proudhon (1809–65), who rejected as eccentric the notions of earlier socialists, regarding the *phalanstères* as romanticized rustic fantasies. Liberty for ordinary people was the principle for the good life; exploitation, inequality and oppression were the bars to this and should be removed. Although sharing the Lockean view that one was entitled to the fruits of one's labour, the expropriation of the work of others was immoral and drew forth his memorable declamation that 'property is theft'.

In fact not all industrialists glorified the harsh logic of the classical economists. Robert Owen (1771–1857) was a self-made industrialist appalled by the conditions imposed upon workers. Believing character to be formed by environment, he thought the workplace should itself function as a community. His New Lanark Mills were run paternalistically, providing the families of workers with housing, health care, shops and education. The experiment aroused great interest; he wrote pamphlets, gave evidence to parliamentary select committees and addressed the US Congress. Yet he roused discomfort in establishment hearts, particularly as he became progressively more inclined towards cooperative production methods.

Marx: the community under capitalism

The most fundamental critique of the liberal individualist vision came from German polymath Karl Marx, the intellectual giant of the modern age. Marx was influenced by Hegel and the earlier socialists, but no modern thinker has a greater claim to have placed his stamp on the intellectual climate of the twentieth century and on the course of real world events. In pointing out the simple, though little appreciated fact that the most important thing for human survival was production of materials, Marx unlocked a social Pandora's box. The new capitalistic mode of production contained profound implications, complications and contradictions for the whole of life. Although Marx is seen as being preoccupied with material things, in that his world is driven by the satisfaction of human wants, he is essentially concerned with the quality of life, declaring in the opening pages of his great work, *Das Kapital*, that 'the nature of the wants, whether . . . they arise in the stomach or in the imagination, does not affect the matter' (Marx 1930: 3).

According to Marx, although citizens may be legally free, they were really bound to the factory-owners who purchased their labour just like any other commodity. While labour was purchased in one market, the things made by the workers were sold in another, so that the price of the product was not related to that of the labour, leaving the employer with a surplus, or profit. Although liberals claimed that each individual had the right to the product of his or her own labour, the capitalist production process was a device for cheating, or exploiting, them. A number of consequences followed from the profit-maximizing goal. These were designed to widen the gap between the price of labour and that of its product, and included starvation wages, long hours, nightmare working conditions, minimal state assistance, a pool of unemployment and so on. It is difficult to imagine a mode of production more provocative, more alienating, or more destructive of any idea of community. For the great mass, the liberal docrine of freedom proves to be just the opposite.

Yet the effects extended beyond civil society, penetrating the state itself. While Hegel idealistically placed the political life of the state above all else, Marx saw the wealth which could be gained in the civil sphere leading to dominance in the political. For the masses, citizenship was reduced to empty symbolism, the vote a worthless chip in a bankrupt casino; the state which was supposed to realize the full potential of all was but a 'committee for managing the affairs of the bourgeoisie'.

Hence Marx identified the most compelling question of the modern era, one which was to engage him throughout his life: how can a fair and just community exist in the context of modern industrial society? Could such a society ever offer the mass the equality and fraternity required for real freedom, as opposed to the bogus freedom of equality before the law?

Although Marx saw early socialists as utopians, his own prescriptions hardly match his profound diagnosis. He regarded the opposition between individual and society as false; like Hegel he saw the individual as entirely shaped by society. There were no natural or divinely ordained inequalities, no natural serfs, slaves, kings, or even nations. His was a broadly Fourierist vision in which work and leisure were not alienated. All would share the personal enrichment which throughout history had been the prerogative of minorities. He believed that the truly communal society, at one with human instinct, would come through a developmental process, driven by the tensions and contradictions of capitalism. The French Revolution had demonstrated what a united people could achieve and Marx saw the great proletariat created by capitalism as a monster which would destroy the economic order to establish a workers' state. Beyond this he envisaged an age of communism, a truly communal way of life in which the state would wither away, a redundant memory of a distant era.

Real world events have not been kind to Marx's predictions. Although often seeming near to collapse, the bourgeois state has managed to hang on, its power to avert revolution clearly underrated. Moreover, those states which did claim to have installed communist regimes did little to realize Marx's idyll. He seems as utopian as those he criticized. It is in the social democratic ideal, enshrined in the 'Labourism' which Marx derided, that modern industrial societies have come closest to realizing the communal life, although none can be said to be untouched by his complex and expansive genius.

Community and citizenship

Citizenship in the modern state

Throughout the history of thought there runs the feeling that people are at their best through membership of a community where the greater interest (whether this be primitive survival needs, the Greek law of nature, the divine law of Christianity, Rousseau's general will, Kant's law of reason, Hegel's divine idea or the state altruism of Green) comes before that of the individual.

The final question is how to give expression to the spirit of community within the modern state. The answer to this can be found in the ancient notion of citizenship invented by the Greeks and reformulated variously through the ages. However, although it offers the key, citizenship has in practice been an exclusive right, reserved to those who are in some way deserving (with property the usual surrogate for virtue). The French Revolution affirmed that true citizenship in modern society must embrace all, yet capitalism can in fact limit effective citizenship by denying to many the resources needed to participate in social life and by placing the state in the hands of the few. English historian and sociologist, Richard Henry Tawney (1880–1962), bringing a strong strain of Christian ethics into the debate, saw the greatest bar to the spirit of community in the gross economic inequalities veining society (Tawney 1931).

Lively argues that, however elusive real world political equality may be, some approximation to it must be a precondition of democracy (1975: 146–7). Effective political equality must be more than a legal right to participate; participation must be genuinely possible through education, good health and material resources. Hence, human rights theorists like Alan Gewirth (1981) and Richard Wasserstrom (1964) argue that citizens must have a right to social and economic well-being. What can be a more fundamental human right than the right to survival (Plant *et al.* 1980). If this is granted it is difficult to deny a universal right to a range of collectively provided services with health care the most fundamental of all.

For many modern writers, including Richard Titmuss, father of the academic study of the welfare state, there is under capitalism a fundamental contradiction: the ideals of citizenship demand equality, while those of capitalism demand inequality. However, as Hegel had argued, the community of individuals could be diverse and differentiated while being morally united, and the state was the supreme vehicle for this. Marshall (1950), who made citizenship a basis of his analysis (see p. 27), believed that the modern state resolves these tensions by promoting a 'hyphenated society', linking the three spheres of democracy, capitalism and welfare. Rather than divide, these promote the social cohesion which capitalism denies by complementing each other. The market is needed to fund state welfare; state welfare is needed to legitimate the market; the essence of the social democratic state is compromise and symbiosis.

However, this compromise remains uneasy. Attacked from left and right, the social democratic state must forever live in tension. During the 1980s the right turned a blind eye to the power of welfare to legitimate and civilize the market and was aided by the defects in the system – the sins of the fathers. However, the result was impoverishment. To survive, the hyphenated social democratic state must incorporate the values of politics.

Community and politics

Individualism, be it methodological or ethical, is of necessity a denial of politics. Politics arises from the very nature of human existence and the instinct to live together, resolving conflicting demands through discussion and compromise rather than market competition. A great number of our important freedoms, including religious toleration, freedom of expression, sexual pluralism and so on, are unrelated to the market or economic prosperity and can only be secured through the processes of politics, a belief that there can be such a thing as a 'national interest and the creation of a political culture which values true and equal liberty for all' (Weale 1990). As Bernard Crick says, politics 'is not just a necessary evil; it is a realistic good. Political activity is a type of moral activity; it is a free activity, and it is inventive, flexible, enjoyable, and human . . .' (1964: 141). When people are working together in harmony they are not sacrificing their individuality, they are expressing it. The individual can only achieve fulfilment in terms of a community. A Mozart can only write if others hear, a Renoir only paint if others will see. Indeed, the free supermarket can only purvey its wares if there are people to enter its self-opening portals and load their chariots from its glowing deep-freezes.

9 RESTORING THE COMMUNAL STATE

Hegel lamented that the owl of Minerva spreads its wings only at the gathering of the dusk; we learn wisdom only when it is too late. The Thatcherite project failed in its ostensible claims: the country is not richer; unemployment has increased; crime has increased; the NHS and the education system are in crisis; the nation has become less healthy; state employees are demoralized, although gagged by government from voicing public criticism; far from being a classless society, inequality has increased to be the greatest since records began (Wilkinson 1991), and the emergence of a shaming new underclass sleeping in the gutters invites derision of the so-called 'trickle-down' effect. There was even failure on the more overtly rightist elements of the agenda: public expenditure has not been rolled back, the total level of taxation has not fallen (although direct tax has been reduced dramatically); the numbers on social security have not fallen and universal child benefit and free education and health care, although under stress, have survived. Most importantly, the quality of people's lives is poorer than in the 1950s and 1960s. Although the logic of individualism was never sustainable, some were taken in, and the wisdom which arrives only at dusk may have come too late for many. Yet politics remains the art of the possible and the sins of the fathers need not be visited upon all the sons. Social democracy is more tenacious than the New Right has imagined (Peterson and Thomas 1986); the communal ideal can be reasserted under the impetus of reason and will.

Socialism is dead, long live socialism

The 1980s heard much boasting from the right that it was they who had made the intellectual running. Many on the left seemed to agree; the state, a cumbersome and wounded leviathan, no longer appeared smart, as trade unions offered members cut-price BUPA membership and the Labour Party conceded, if not extolled, the virtues of privatization, even weakening an earlier commitment to reclaim to the state the highly symbolic water industry (*The Times*, 14 November 1991). In December 1991, *Marxism Today*, despite its name a clarion of social democracy, published its final issue. Would its successor be *Marxism Yesterday*? Truly the core of the social democratic world seemed to be melting down.

We have been told by the New Right that the world has changed, that socialism is dead. Its demise has been a long and painful process, with many of the nearest and dearest unwilling to face the seriousness of the illness, showing a brave face and praying for remission. Even when it appeared to lie grey and unbreathing, there were those who turned a blind eye to the flat trace of the cardiograph, while others sought comfort from the story of Lazarus. However, the acceptance by the Eastern Bloc countries not only that the body is pronounced brain dead, but that the heart no longer beats, ends all hope. To be sure, political regimes and parties continue to sail under the socialist emblem, but it is a flag of convenience; they can prosper and gain adherents only to the extent that they avoid any real commitment to the ideology they profess. Today, to advocate socialism would suggest an unhealthy leaning towards necrophilia.

But what can this death really signify? The living can know little of the world beyond the grave. Some frail vessels may have become exhausted, faltered, and been discredited, but the soul of socialism, which is its pure essence, lives on in the unquenchable spirit of community: the conviction that a meaningful life for people can only take place in an atmosphere of fellowship and harmony with others. The ethical ideal remains relevant just as the ethics of Christianity survived the excesses of the Crusades, the Reformation and Counter-Reformation.

We must remember that what the Thatcher revolution sought to 'bury' was not the socialism of Eastern Europe. These were not communal systems; lack of democracy denied citizenship to ordinary people and they were already on a self-destruct course, their immolation forecast by the left more than the right. What Thatcherism attacked was the sapling social democracy which sought not to abolish the market, but to humanize it.

It was frequently said that the zeal of the New Right led to shootings in the foot in various particular ways, most notably in the case of the poll tax. Yet in truth the New Right assault on the state represents general self-mutilation on an heroic scale. Under social democracy the private and public realms exist in a symbiosis (today it is fashionable to speak of this as the social market), enabling capitalism to improve its face and avoid its inherent tendencies to crisis. The social democratic state evolved organically rather than through revolution, its complex architecture, like that of a cathedral, created over many years. The forces of the New Right thought it fragile and easily destroyed, yet the policy of bringing in the constitutional bulldozers contains a fatal simplicity. Without social concern where is the moral force to mitigate the market? This chapter asks the most fundamental questions of all: how profound is the damage and how is it to be repaired?

Assessing the damage: is the community dead?

Thatcher's great 'hegemonic project' was intended to create a dominant ideology condensing a wide range of popular post-war discontents around an authoritarian programme (Jessop et al. 1988: 68–124). Much government rhetoric proclaimed the rebirth of the competitive spirit of national get-up-and-go and the Yuppie emerged as the icon of the new age. Yet only politicians could proclaim such national-scale Pauline conversion. The Conservative success was always in considerable measure a creation of an electoral system offering disproportionate misrepresentation rather than a grand renunciation of consensus values by an entire population.

After over a decade of the 'no such thing as' society, how content are ordinary people? This question is not one which the apostles of the new individualism are entitled to evade; it is the most important that can be asked, the key which opens all philosophical debate. J. K. Galbraith (1958) had added a phrase to the language of politics in the late 1950s when he castigated a capitalist world of 'private affluence and public squalor'. His Cassandra words appear to have been prophetic as well as apposite in their time.

Social research published in the popular as well as the academic press pointed to the conclusion that Thatcherism was 'a crusade that failed'. At the level of base materialism, those who have been made unemployed, or the members of the new underclass, are clear losers. But where is the benefit for the comfortable middle classes who, with fatter wallets, find their roads pot-holed, their streets litter strewn, their cultural life debased, and the schools of their children dilapidated and without books? What comfort is there in knowing that hospital wards are closing and the only answer is to reinvest tax savings in private insurance schemes? Who amongst the well-heeled in the supermarket can feel other than a deep sense of unease that the boxes they leave empty will become the homes of others? People who were not personally poorer still lamented the public squalor and wanted higher public service expenditure, higher taxation and a more compassionate state.

This was confirmed in the eighth annual survey of British social attitudes carried out by the independent organization, Social and Community Planning Research (Jowell et al. 1991), which revealed near universal, cross-class backing for the NHS, with support for the Thatcherite preference for individual insurance falling. Perhaps most striking of all was the fact that support for more public spending with higher taxes was found to have risen from around 33 per cent of the population to over half. Only 3 per cent believed that taxes and welfare state spending should be cut. Moreover, while 38 per cent wanted more spending on health care and 28 per cent more on education, despite post-Gulf-war euphoria only 2 per cent favoured greater defence expenditure. It was possible to discern palpable evidence of a post-materialist ethos in a people grown weary of the casino capitalism. Thatcher's successor, John Major, was forced to renounce the past and speak the language of community in the 1992 election campaign.

Meddlesome priests

Amongst the most vehement of the sceptics were the custodians of the nation's ethical life. Although a Protestant work ethic sustained the bourgeoisie throughout the nineteenth century, the Anglican Church was troubled and no longer willing to see itself as the Conservative Party at prayer. Various prelates, including David Jenkins, Bishop of Durham, and David Shepherd, Bishop of Liverpool, spoke out. Robert Runcie, as Archbishop of Canterbury, set up an enquiry into Britain's urban problems and its report, *Faith in the City*, was a crushing indictment (Church of England 1985). Thatcher's successor could do nothing to stem the tide, which became ecumenical. In 1991, the new Archbishop of Canterbury, George Carey, castigated the conditions of the poor, his words echoed by Cardinal Basil Hume, the Catholic Archbishop of Westminster, who added a tirade against education policy. Ironically, a number of New Right politicians are ostentatiously pious in the Christian faith, apparently immune to the inconsistency and untroubled at the thought of negotiating the eye of the needle.

Poll axed

Notwithstanding the wide front on which the New Right assailed social democracy, the most spectacular sortie was the poll tax. This was the most singular expression of Thatcherism imaginable, combining tax cuts for the rich, monumental contempt for common people, hatred of the state in general and for local government in particular. Unlike the entirely non-progressive VAT which had risen insidiously, the poll tax wore no fig leaf, its unfairness in brazen display. Thatcher, upon meeting her *pons asinorum* was, as ever, resolute, but the party's backbenchers, fearful of an embarrassing nemesis at the polling booths, reckoned that her shelf-life had expired; it became possible to think that a tragedy had reached its finale.

No man is an island: everybody needs good neighbours

Yet the hype continues into the 1990s, although the triumphalism sounds increasingly hollow. The case for humanity and a communal view of life is infinitely more profound, embedded in ordinary speech, in the music and the arts, and in the essential Christian ethic underlying western civilization. During the 1980s popular songs continued to extol the virtues of love, rather than choice, competition or money, and the signature theme to Britain's most popular soap opera propagated a subversive message: 'Everybody needs good neighbours'.

The communal life is more attuned to the mature instinct; in so far as the entirely selfish person exists, he or she could only be regarded as disturbed, maladjusted and emotionally arrested. Freud, Mead and Piaget, in their various ways, all depicted human development as a progression from a childhood preoccupation with the self to the recognition of the existence and claims of others. For normal people the sense of community is necessary to fulfilment; in 1624, when the long-lived Hobbes was a stripling of 36 years, John Donne wrote in his *Devotions*: 'No man is an Island, entire in itself; every man is a piece of a Continent, a part of the main.'

Hence, although the foliage of the tree of social democracy may look acid-rain damaged, the roots remain sufficiently well embedded for renewed growth. How is this to be accomplished? Can social democracy be restored in more hardy form than before? Can a communal state be created in which the values of ancient citizenship can offer modern people the good life that the Athenian aristocrats sought? Discussion of this must form the heart of debate in the 1990s; we must consider rebuilding the communal culture, the welfare state, the communal economy and the machinery of the communal state.

Changing our minds: the communal culture

We have stressed the importance of the psychological dimension in the New Right's hegemonic project – the reinforcing of an individualist 'common sense' about life in the popular consciousness. Although the social democratic state can take modern capitalist society closest to the communal ideal, it can only thrive within the context of a communal political culture. Can this be revived after the New Right mind assault? It is clear from the social survey evidence that it can; indeed the Thatcher design to eradicate it was really the more audacious project, challenging as it did our fundamental instinct towards community.

What are the values which the social democratic society should hold dear; what should be the 'common sense' of social democracy? In contemplating the reconstruction of the communal political culture we can do no worse than return to the ageless desiderata which have inspired the legendary quest for social justice and which will always be prime casualties of the individualist assault: equality, fraternity and liberty.

Not equal but egalitarian

During the 1980s Britain not only became a more unequal society, the government deliberately fostered an inegalitarian political culture. The rich were urged to cast off the sense of bourgeois guilt engendered in the consensus era and to flaunt their success – their fast Prussian cars and oriental car phones. It was argued that inequality was the key to initiative. The egalitarian argument is subject to much parody and much refutation by *reductio ad adsurdum* (only a fool would claim that people are equal in their endowments). The major modern statement on egalitarianism was made by Tawney (1931), who agreed that any idea that all were entirely equal in character and intelligence was 'romantic illusion'. However, the mark of the civilized society should be the elimination of those differences caused by the organization of society. The right have no difficulty in agreeing that the law should treat everyone equally. Why then should not the state take it upon itself to treat them equally in other great matters of existence, such as health and education?

More important than the utopian idea of an *equal society* is that of an *egalitarian culture*, which regards equality of treatment and opportunity as an ethical goal towards which policies should always move. The egalitarian political culture is a precondition of the communal society. How is it to be brought about? Crosland (1956) argued that a precondition of any strategy to equalize incomes was economic growth. This was based on the argument that the rich would be unwilling to see their absolute standards fall, but that they could live with a little levelling up. Yet Thatcher took a contrary view: inequality was cherished on the grounds that it was actually good for everyone. While Crosland had argued that growth would lead to reduced inequality, Thatcher asserted that inequality would lead to growth. The problem with the Crosland position is that the absence of economic growth rules out policies promoting equality. Moreover, it is a position reaffirmed by Neil Kinnock in the manifesto of his new designer party, *Meet the Challenge, Make the Change*, which promises that increased public spending will only come from increased growth: 'We will not spend, nor will we promise to spend, more than the country can afford' (Labour Party 1989). But can we not argue for equality without growth? The answer in the communal society must certainly be 'yes'. The justification comes from the altruistic urge within people, the cold logic of utilitarianism and the precept at the heart of communitarian belief – social justice.

Altruism

There is no real justification for believing that the better-off cannot altruistically accept redistribution. In Sweden, the home of social democracy, the blue-collar trade union movement (LO) has long practised a policy of minimizing wage differentials through sacrifices by workers in more prosperous industries. However, only a communal culture can condone this. Better-paid workers are unlikely to welcome sacrifices for their poorer brothers and sisters in a society permeated by privilege and topped by a glittering aristocracy. In Scandinavia we do not find golden coaches pulled by a train of white horses, but bicycling monarchies, not the joke the British like to claim, but a great communal symbol.

Utilitarianism

Contrary to New-Right-think, it can be argued that an egalitarian society is a precondition of economic growth. Many of the pleasures of the rich are in their essential nature dependent not upon absolute wealth, but upon inequality. For example, the joy of the exclusive golf club is that the fairways are protected from the hordes. The advantages conferred by a public school education, or private health care, are in the same category. Hirsch (1976) sees the British economy as a 'positional' one in which status, position and privilege are preserved by processes of exclusion. The 'positional economy' makes possible the 'conspicuous consumption' and 'conspicuous leisure' identified by Thorstein Veblen (1970), wherein the rich need to make ritual display of their distinctiveness. From the great system of ancient public schools to the director's dining room, British society is replete with examples.

Another utilitarian argument comes from the surprising discovery that inequality, rather like smoking, is bad for the health. Research by the Centre for Medical Research at the University of Sussex reveals that amongst affluent nations, where obviously life-damaging poverty does not exist, there is an astonishingly strong correlation between health (including life expectancy) and inequality. Thus the US, Luxemburg and (West) Germany, although twice as rich in per capita terms as Greece and Spain, had lower life expectancies. As a country reduces its income inequality, so the general standards of health improve; this is the reason why Japanese life expectancy has surged ahead of the rest of the world. At the same time, in Britain the Chief Medical Officer at the Department of Health reported in 1989 that death rates for men and women in the 15–45 age group had been rising since 1985 as Britain became a more unequal society (see p. 32). Hence it must be concluded that the psychological damage done to a society through inequality creates disease-inducing, life-shortening stress; the quantity as well as the quality of life is impaired (Wilkinson 1991).

Social justice

Social justice has very little place in the hearts and minds of individualists, the fixation with rights of possession denying any basis for redistribution. Yet a policy of egalitarianism is easily justified on social justice grounds. In the first place, it can be demonstrated that any idea that present wealth distribution reflects ability is wild falsehood; if this were so then a graph should resemble the normal distribution characteristic of intelligence test results, which it manifestly does not. For example, in 1985 the top 5 per cent of the population owned 40 per cent of UK wealth (*Social Trends* 1988: Table 5.21). Generally speaking, the rich are rich because of the social cooperation which constitutes the community. They gain a right to hold their property because others consent to go without; the poor are indeed 'ragged-trousered philanthropists'. Hence the community is being extremely kind to the rich and it is in their interests to ensure its survival.

Of course, inherited wealth is even more provocative. In Britain, as nowhere else in the world, it is honoured in the fully fledged aristocracy displayed in stately country house museums throughout the land they largely own. Yet what is preserved is a pattern of distribution inherited from an age of naked greed and brutality. It gives a strong moral case for resistance and even violence, as in Carl Sandburg's menacing poem quoted in *The New Internationalist* (June 1991: 9):

> Get off this estate.
> What for?
> Because it's mine.
> Where did you get it?
> From my father.
> Where did he get it?
> From his father.
> And where did he get it?
> He fought for it.
> Well, I'll fight you for it.

We may put the boot on the other foot and claim that it is really more valid not to try to justify equality but to ask its opponents to justify inequality. Locke had a version of the bogus trickle-down effect (see p. 69) and Nozick's deontological justification is that the removal of inequality, however good the intention, infringes more fundamental rights (see p. 83). Radical liberal philosopher John Rawls (1973) looks for a redistributive conception of social justice. Inequalities must be regarded as unjust in principle and require special pleading. They can only be justified if they contribute to the advantage of the least well off, and the positions and offices of those advantaged according to this principle must be genuinely open to all. These are the questions which the egalitarian society would ask. Inequality, rather than being obsequiously venerated in an unregeneratedly deferential political culture, must be robustly challenged and asked to justify itself at every turn. Does the immense wealth of, say, the Duke of Westminster, make the poorest in society better off than they would otherwise be? Much existing inequality in Britain would need a very good lawyer to survive in this court.

The joyless society

What of the argument intoned from the right that the egalitarian society will impose a dull regimentation on our lives? Those lucky enough to become full-time students have, for a brief period, a taste of enforced levelling imposed by the Universities Funding Council and the hall-of-residence canteen. Yet how many people lament their student days as dull humourless years? Whether spent at the Oxford Union, the Footlights Club, the pool table in the redbrick bar or the Poly disco, for most people it is treasured as a halcyon period, becoming progressively rose tinted as the years go by. Far from dull uniformity, student life can foster colourful diversity and creativity; blacks can come in, gays can come out, sons of dustmen can push in the scrum with scions of the aristocracy and daughters of duchesses can serve instant coffee to nervous boys from comprehensives. If it is dull uniformity that the right fear, let them pull down the high-rise flats and the countless rows of terraced and semi-detached hutches which furrow the landscape. Here are the monuments to the unequal society, tributes to the trickle-down effect.

Equality and growth: the other side of the coin

We have argued that there is a case for equality even under conditions where economic growth is not available to finance redistribution painlessly. However, it is possible to go further to argue that equality can itself promote growth. The idea of positional goods and conspicuous consumption speaks of waste and profligacy. The exclusion practices necessary to maintain inequality rob the nation of the full development of its intellectual capacity, while conspicuous consumption diverts wealth from investment. Moreover, the feelings of envy deliberately engendered disrupt labour relations within industry and block economic adjustment (Hindess and Hirst 1983).

Fraternity: he ain't heavy

Fraternity lies at the heart of the concept of community. It is the very antithesis of egoistic individualism and before it the market and public choice models must collapse like houses of cards. Tawney (1931) argued that fraternity provides the moral integration of society, a view reinforced in the context of modern Britain by Halsey (1978).

Although the story of Cain and Abel is not good PR for fraternity, the notion that all are siblings deflects any charge of sloppy, impractical sentimentality. Such relationships are characterized by rigour, and indeed rivalry; from pillow fights in childhood, brothers may go on to chase the same girl, sisters the same boy. They will also tell each other uncomfortable home truths and condemn bad behaviour, but in their hearts they know they are of the same blood. They will encourage and support, bestow gifts rather than barter, donate kidneys and, *in extremis*, will sacrifice their lives. In the fraternal society welfare is the right of all; the well off accept the need for taxation and many important goods and services are provided not as market transactions, but as gifts.

Indeed, the gift relationship idea was extensively developed by Richard Titmuss (1970), who took blood donation as a dramatic illustration of the moral and utilitarian superiority of the gift over the commercial transaction. When an individual gives blood the action is done not for the self, but for the good of the community, but when it is sold it is no more than an egoistic act. In a grim forewarning of the horror of the HIV-infected blood that was to reach British haemophiliacs from the US, he asserted the moral and physical threat of commercial blood banks for both donors and recipients.

Gift relationships such as donations to charity and bequests upon death express the fraternal culture and produce cohesion, whereas market exchanges, into which individuals enter only for gain, have a fragmentary effect. Hence in a modern society a substantial leavening of gift relationships can counteract the market. The state provides the only effective basis for achieving this on a significant scale (Boulding 1973). Opportunities are boundless, including direct gifts such as student grants, income maintenance payments and pensions, and gifts in kind such as health care, housing and education. Indeed, the vexed issue of taxation can itself be addressed in terms of the gift relationship. Instead of the Nozickian position that tax is nothing less than daylight robbery, it can be argued that it is state-orchestrated giving. Indeed, this is a far more expedient and legitimate form of giving than is the charitable donation. Even those who would avoid an encounter with the importunate lady with the collecting box in the high street will consent to give through tax in the knowledge that others must do the same.

Liberty: born free, but everywhere in chains

Liberty is by no means the prerogative of individualists and classical liberals; it was the central concern of organic thinkers such as Rousseau and Hegel, is developed by modern communitarian thinkers such as Sandel (1984), and is flagged up in the practical manifestos of contemporary politicians of the left such as Roy Hattersley (*Choose Freedom*, 1987) and Brian Gould (*Socialism and Freedom*, 1985). Although trumpeting the idea of freedom, the New Right speaks only of the absence of state interference in the economy. However, freedom can be endangered by agencies other than the state; for the poor the market itself denies freedom in a profound and fundamental way.

Thus, in the matter of liberty under capitalism the state has a positive rather than a negative role; it must actively bestow freedom upon citizens by mitigating those forces which would curtail it. This can easily be characterized by the right as the big-brother role, but in fact all liberties ultimately depend upon positive state action. The free market is neither free nor a market without the strong state conferring rights and opportunities. Indeed, it would be difficult for the class which owns most of the country to do so without an extremely benevolent 'welfare of the propertied' state.

How do we change our minds?

'Achieving a comprehensive social strategy . . . represents a challenge to our whole society . . . if we are to live in a truly civilised society' (Piachaud 1991: 224).

Rousseau and J. S. Mill were, in their different ways, conscious of the need to educate people into communal ways of thinking. Gramsci (1971) warns of the power of the capitalist bourgeoisie, living by the precepts of individualism, to shape the mass mind in sympathy with bourgeois interests. How does the social democratic state educate its members and combat the hegemonic forces of the right? In part the answer was provided by the Thatcher government, which spent hundreds of millions of pounds on advertising the virtues of privatization; Sid of British Gas and Beatie of British Telecom became household names. Today advertising is amongst the world's mega-industries; the modern social democractic state must be able to explain itself to its citizens. The provision of such information cannot be left to the pompous bureau-speak of the mandarins, nor entrusted to sloganizing political parties. An independent public agency should use the slick, glossy techniques of Madison Avenue to sell not the nationalized industries, but the ideas of social democracy.

The welfare state: the heart of the community

The values of equality, fraternity and liberty can only be entrenched through the formal machinery of a welfare state. Whatever the New Right may claim, any market society, necessarily creating losers and winners, requires state welfare. However, a machinery for providing for life's failures is not a communitarian force; it is a kind of state charity, as enshrined in the nineteenth-century Poor Law mentality, and as cold as that of the private variety. Services provided on this basis are open to the scrounger critique, and those who fund the system will nurture the grudge that they are exploited. In the communitarian society, the welfare state must be defended in more robust terms. In the first place it is possible to meet the utilitarians head on; there is a good utilitarian case for the welfare state. Beyond this we can speak the language of fraternity and justice, and finally there is the fundamental value of citizenship, the essential ingredient of the good life, perhaps the most secure justification of all.

Welfare as utilitarianism

Although rejecting the idea of natural rights, Bentham stood well within the liberal tradition in the belief that the maximum happiness of the greatest number could only be obtained through the pain–pleasure calculations of atomistic individuals. Hence, state intervention in the market is only ruled out because it might be expected to reduce the total sum of happiness. Yet by dispensing with natural rights there was no real (ontological) argument for a sacred private realm into which the state could not enter, no reason why liberty should remain the prime ethical desideratum. If rational governments could see a way of increasing the total sum of utility through state welfare programmes, then they were logically bound to act, even if this restricted liberty (Gamble 1981: 80). Hence, arch Benthamite Edwin Chadwick was able to justify large public health expenditure measures in his great nineteenth-century sanitation movement.

Not only does this justify state intervention, it justifies paying for it. It can be argued that the possible loss of self-respect, life chances, material goods and so on consequent upon poverty obviously outweighs the potential loss of happiness experienced by taxpayers. In the former case, the ability to participate fully is clearly impaired, while in the latter it is almost certainly not. The logic of the argument moves inexorably on to justify progressive taxation.

Welfare as fraternity and justice

The welfare state is also an expression of the cherished communal value of fraternity. A flaw in the scrounger argument that people are responsible for their own predicaments (the lazy who have no jobs, and the smokers and drinkers who become ill) is that few of us can say that we never have, and never will, behave foolishly, and when we do we need help. As a family rallies round those in trouble, including its black sheep, so the communal society should support its weaker brothers and sisters. The fraternal ideal can also justify the necessary taxation since payment becomes an expression of Hegel's universal altruism, the spirit of love found in the family extended to society at large.

The welfare state also finds easy justification in terms of social justice. Empirical researchers such as Townsend repeatedly demonstrate that most of those in need are unfortunate victims of the bewildering economic system which sweeps them along like weightless corks on the tide. They are bearing the community's cost of economic adjustment, often in the form of unemployment, and there is no moral justification for expecting them to do this without compensation. In this case, the taxation required, far from being robbery, is merely balancing the books. Interestingly, the post-war nationalization programme which dispossessed the coal and railway magnates did not ask them to shoulder the burden of economic adjustment without handsome state recompense.

Welfare as a right of citizenship

A bedrock of the communitarian welfare state is the idea of citizenship. People receive welfare services in order to realize a right to full citizenship; consequently the services themselves are to be seen as rights of citizenship. In this the welfare state is fundamentally an egalitarian force, for there can be no real citizenship without the notion of equal participation by all. While it could never be expected to create an entirely equal society, it makes a reality of claims that all should have the same chance of enjoying the normal life of the community. Grounding state welfare in the idea of equal membership of the community makes it possible to argue in the liberal language of rights, which in turn preserves the dignity necessary for true citizenship, since people can stand up for their rights rather than petition for charity (Harris 1987: Ch. 8). Moreover, the idea of welfare as a right of citizenship is actually quite consistent with a responsibility of individuals for their own lives and can undermine the paternalistic tendencies in state welfare provision.

Indeed, this notion of preserving dignity argues for a certain kind of welfare state, one in which services are provided in kind (education and health care) rather than in cash (to pre-empt the scrounger accusation) and are available on a universal (non-stigmatizing) basis rather than a selective one. The citizenship view also gives a moral justification for paying for welfare through taxation since, by definition, citizenship must be understood to carry obligations.

The state of freedom
Hence the welfare state is the practical embodiment of the sense of positive freedom
to act, rather than the freedom of being left alone. To be left alone in a jungle of
wild beasts is not a situation to be sought by any rational being. The communal state
enables people to participate, making a reality of the idea of choice which is falsely
supposed to be embodied in the market. Education, income, health and housing
are the means through which we become free to participate in the life of the
community – the essence of citizenship. There can be no communal state under
capitalism without a citizenship-based welfare state.

The communal economy

The communal state must not be concerned merely with welfare through the
distribution of wealth; it must have a hand in wealth production, going beyond
demand management to influence the supply side of the macroeconomic
equation.

The justice-seeking economy
To remain buoyant a capitalist economy must be constantly changing, seeking new
products, new markets and, most of all, new technologies. This process redistributes
income, wealth and power and poses profound moral questions for a society
(Thurrow 1981). Generally the purpose of new technology is to reduce the labour
component of production; those who have invested their lives in the development of
an outmoded skill are asked to bear the cost of industrial change while others reap
the benefits. If not ragged-trousered, they are asked to be blue-collared philanthropists; not unnaturally they may be expected to resist.

The New Right argue that market outcomes are automatically just, but this masks
the essentially political problem. Ironically, potential losers may attempt to use
their own market power to resist change (Olson 1982) so that the market-favouring
government will itself want to intervene, forcing the market to work one way rather
than another. Whether it crushes resistance, as in the print-workers' and miners'
strikes in the 1980s, or shoulders the costs through welfare, the problem lands at
the door of the state. It is not the role of the communal state to crush its citizens or
label them, as did Thatcher, 'the enemy within'. Only in a harmonious society,
not riven by differences of wealth and class, can the losers and gainers strike a
bargain in which the distributional effects of economic change are modified for the
good of all.

However, the communal state cannot be content merely to support market
victims; if the interests of the community are to be placed above the self-interest of
the capitalist class, it must go further. This it does by becoming entrepreneurial.

The entrepreneurial community
Ten people in a workshop will not become a pin factory. A private firm does not
operate internally on *laissez-faire* principles; it is organized and managed to ensure a
rational use of resources. In this sense the firm is an economic community. Why
then should a state be different? The Hayekian answer to this is that in the first place

central management is impossibly complex and in the second it will lead to totalitarianism. Interestingly, the right is untroubled by the totalitarianism and crushing of the human spirit within the firm.

Modern writers of the left, accepting Hayek's broad point that the volume of information required would be much too great and unmanageable, do not claim that a national economy could be run as a command economy (Hodgson 1984: 74–5). However, it is equally naive to imagine that the market is a smooth and efficient transmitter of information; it is crude, unreliable and uncaring, a parasitic creeper winding itself around its host society, drawing upon its life sap. Yet ultimately it strangles the host and so dies itself.

What's to be done?

While the British tradition, following Smith, saw international trade as traffic between individual firms operating across national boundaries, others saw it as competition between states, a view which led governments to assume a new kind of mercantilist role. There is much to be learned from this. The examples of Britain's main rivals demonstrate that the communal economy does not entail a Hayekian nightmare of overcentralized, overbearing, overbureaucratized government condemning people to a 'new serfdom'. In the 1970s and 1980s, for example, Sweden and Austria weathered the end of long boom by simultaneously holding down inflation and unemployment while managing to maintain an enviable record of economic growth. All was achieved by corporatist methods and in a climate in which civil and political freedom flourished (Weale 1990: 522).

The economy can be conducted like an orchestra so that the community, through its government, decides which instruments shall be blown loudest, which shall be muted, and when the symbols should clash; the players are persuaded as well as instructed and can voice their own opinions to the conductor. In the *laissez-faire* orchestra of the New Right each performer decides when and how to play and chooses his or her own tune. However good the intentions of the players, and however fine their instruments, the result is not the sublime harmony of Hayek's spontaneous order but a raucous cacophony.

The machinery of community

While it is true that the communal culture lies in the minds of people rather than in institutions, it is in the latter that we see the tangible expression of community values and their protection. Despite sponsorship of the arts and sport, or grandiose advertising of soft drinks purporting to unite the youth of the world, the reconstruction of the community cannot come from the market; it is pre-eminently the function of the state which is, as Aristotle said, the highest form of community. Yet the communal society cannot exist in the bad state, in a state where the democratic institutions are mere display (dignified elements as the elitist Bagehot said) or where the state officials cannot see themselves as custodians of the community interest. We need to consider both the constitution and the state machinery.

The constitution

Constitutional reforms are rarely far from the political agenda; they were placed to the forefront during the New Right era as citizenship plunged into crisis (signalling, for example, the rise of the Charter 88 movement) and Thatcher revealed the alarming fault lines in the constitution, particularly the almost complete absence of restraint on the effective power of the prime minister.

The very heart of the democratic process in Britain is anti-communal: the electoral system is not only profoundly unfair to third parties, it abhors coalitions. With a homoeostatic instinct for bipartisan politics it seems designed to endorse the Marxian scenario of unremitting class warfare. Even the seating arrangements in the House of Commons are confrontational while, in the preservation of the House of Lords, Parliament enshrines a culture of caste, class and patronage.

Reformers agree that British citizens should be protected by a Bill of Rights; John Major's Citizens' Charter of 1991 was nothing more than a kind of consumer association stick with which to berate the *bête noire* of the right, the public bureaucrat. The notion of citizens' rights must extend beyond the number of cones on motorways; people who disagree with the New Right do not want their phones tapped by MI5 or their photographs taken by the police. A simple solution to this lacuna is to incorporate into UK law the provisions of the European Convention on Human Rights.

Serving the communal ethic

Hegel, state apologist extraordinaire, saw the bureaucracy as having an absolutely crucial role in promoting the communal interest transcending political interests. Matthew Arnold noted how British culture, with its stress on the right of individuals to do as they like, differed not only from the notion of the state in antiquity, but from that found on the Continent where 'the nation in its collective and corporate character, [is] entrusted with stringent powers for the general advantage in the name of an interest wider than that of individuals' (Stone 1980: 35).

The machinery of the modern state is infinitely complex in its details and its study consigned to a subdiscipline of political science – Public Administration – which labours under the reputation of being boring. Yet despite the efforts of worthy academics to avoid overexciting their readers, the study is, in principle, the very opposite of boring, since it is directly concerned with the machinery which shapes the quality of our lives.

The reputation derives from the liberal doctrine of the neutral state, the belief that bureaucrats are faceless political eunuchs skilled in the art of serving two party masters. Civil servants like to allude to their silky minds and their impartial though aloof sang-froid, employing much imagery of the obedient Rolls-Royce, ready to purr into motion whether the foot on the accelerator is clad in boots or patent leather. It is a particularly functional image for those who have something to gain from remaining outside the glare of the spotlight. Indeed, British public administration is amongst the most secretive in the world – a bureaucratic freemasonry of the great and the good conducting silent rites in a universe of

Whitehall, Horse Guards Parade and the exclusive London clubs. In reality the idea of the neutral bureaucrat is an impossible dream. Few would disagree that in totalitarian states bureaucrats are part of the machinery of repression. Consequently, in the social democratic state they must be expected to serve the citizenship ethic, as judges serve the law.

Contrary to New Right thinking, private sector managerial practices cannot provide the model for modern state administration because, despite superficial similarities, the public domain is profoundly different from the private sector. The basic *raison d'être* of the latter is profit maximization. Although there may be short-term goals such as appeasing political movements concerned with, say, the environment, sponsoring sporting events, or even promoting brass bands, the great edifice of neo-classical economic theory is erected upon premises of individualistic self-interest and, for firms, be they corner-shops or multinationals, this means the never-ending hunt for profit.

Ranson and Stewart argue that public sector management practices 'belong to that domain alone and cannot be resolved by models of organization and management built for the private domain. To each his own' (1989: 24). Public administration must display a particular sense of mission (Waldo 1971; Marini 1973), seeking to facilitate the complex of functions unique to the state, including the following:

1 identifying and balancing conflicting demands in decision-making;
2 informing the public without political bias;
3 voicing the demands of latent groups;
4 facilitating and encouraging participation;
5 constructing compromise solutions to maximize consent;
6 safeguarding citizens' rights;
7 promoting social justice in the allocation of goods and services;
8 promoting social integration;
9 preserving ethical standards in administration.

Generally, the state servants must own a responsibility for promoting *civitas*, a sense of community spirit, thereby facilitating and serving social democracy. The job must carry a sense of vocation and those lacking this need not apply.

Staffing the state
Who are the people to preserve the communal state? The answer must surely be ordinary people selected on the basis of intelligence and aptitude rather than breeding. In its higher (politically significant) ranks the British civil service cannot remain socially elitist, male dominated, and with mandarins' skins as snow white as their collars. Not only is there little reason to swallow the argument that existing recruitment practices secure the best brains, there is doubt as to whether the nature of the job requires the celebrated Rolls-Royce mind. The state should be in hands of those who really know society. Those controlling education should have spent at least some of their time, not desporting on the fabled Eton playing fields, or exerting themselves between Putney and Mortlake, but sitting at the desks of the nation's comprehensives. They should know the inconvenience of outdated textbooks, insufficient equipment and teacher shortages. Similarly, should not those

running the health service know the experience of sitting with a loved one in pain on the waiting list and hearing the supercilious call to the consulting room? It must be remembered that the recruitment pattern was carefully shaped to give power to a certain class; this cannot be logically right for the communal state.

The belief that those responsible for delivering policies ought to have empathy with ordinary people means that recruitment should be genuinely open to both sexes and all social classes and ethnic groups (perhaps underlined with a quota system). The idea of an ethos of public service elevates the importance of education and training. This should include study in the substantive areas to be administered (foreign relations, the economy, education, the welfare state) and disciplines concerned with the wider context and purposes of the social democratic state (ethics, politics, philosophy, sociology and even modern subjects like media studies and women's studies). Most importantly, the 'one of us' theory of personnel management should be abandoned before it becomes a new convention of the constitution, destroying any possibility of developing a public service ethos.

The local state

Hegel advocated intermediate associations which would themselves be incorporated into the state apparatus and bind the community. There is no more ingenious institution within the state for creating a real sense of community than democratic local government; it alone permits ordinary people to be involved with decision-making. However, the rejuvenation of local democracy must go beyond local elections. To be real it must entail responsibility for major functions (social services, education, police, transportation, care of the environment and so on), otherwise the municipalities become no more than hollow cyphers. Moreover, they should have genuine ability to shape policy in their areas without overbearing central government control. This would give our overcentralized constitution a degree of separation of powers. Local autonomy could be enshrined in a written constitution or the abandonment of the *ultra vires* principle could bestow upon local authorities general competence to provide those services their communities desire.

Of course social services are labour intensive and, while there can be no substitute for well-paid and well-trained workers in the field, there is a case for the increased formal involvement of ordinary people on a voluntary basis (Piachaud 1991). Some, including Prince Charles and Labour's Michael Meacher, have argued for a kind of national service but, however organized, there is a large amount of relatively unskilled work in the caring services and the involvement of citizens in giving not their money, but their time to serving the community would be a morally integrating force, generally increasing understanding of the nature of the state's caring role. The present idea that such work should be allocated to offenders for penal reasons is of course absurd, if not an obscene denigration of the concept of community.

Reason and the individual: restoring the faith

Finally comes the dimension of the mind. Not only must bureaucrats sense their ethical purpose, the petit bourgeois, anti-statist view which the public choice theorists elevated to the status of political analysis needs to be expunged from the culture (Goodin 1982). Bureaucrats must not be the butt of tea-drinking jokes. Faith in the technological fix needs renewing; without this we become prey to dark metaphysical forces and ideologies (including those of the free market).

Faith in the professional must also be restored. Without professionalism health care and education must return to the dark ages. Much of the New Right espousal of managerialism was really a mission to undermine the ideal of professionalism. Doctors, nurses, teachers, social workers and so on would tend to put the needs of those depending upon them before considerations of cost (including their own salaries) and the managers were put there to bring them to heel. The derision of professionalism was of course part of this general strategy. Yet, when we are sick or in need of instruction it is not the managers who will treat us or give us comfort. If our house is on fire we will not thank them for saving water.

However, a more important consequence of restoring faith in reason lies in the way we conceive the individual in society. It is no part of this argument that the ultimate ends of society are to be determined in terms of some Burkean mystical conservatism which argues that *what is*, must be what is best. The ultimate ends of existence must be questioned continually; it can never be complacently assumed that they are immutable. Yet such questioning can only take place in a society which encourages free thought and expression. These are the really important freedoms required by individuals. The narrow conception of freedom promoted by the New Right denies the right to make such choices; the ends are predetermined in terms of the inexorable laws of the market – profit and utility maximization. Liberals in the humane tradition, including J. S. Mill, Rousseau, Kant, Rawls and Dworkin, insist upon the moral responsibility of individuals to make choices at the more fundamental levels.

In such a society respect for the individual goes well beyond the right to sell your second-hand car to whoever will pay your price. It entails respect for the rights and dignity of individuals and groups who deviate in some way or other from the communal norm, say in terms of race or sexual preference. There is nothing in the idea of communitarian values which insists upon blind conformity to common norms. Indeed, it is inconceivable that such a society could be cohesive. That the New Right vision of liberalism should lead to an oppressive, class-dominated society, intolerant of minorities, is testimony to the fact that, in resuscitating the ideas of the eighteenth and nineteenth centuries, it is blind to genuinely liberal values.

Sisyphean politics

Many on the left found in Margaret Thatcher much to admire, feeling that the legendary 'resolution' could be profitably emulated by a Labour government, that radical reforms could be secured by the left if the strength of purpose is there. Yet this is a profoundly simplistic reading of modern politics in industrial society. The elected leaders hold office but the reality of power remains mysterious. Behind the politics of office lies the politics of influence, dark *éminences grises* hover in the shadows around the throne. Governments cannot pull levers and make things happen like the driver of a constitutional bulldozer. Moreover, the greatest of the shadowy forces are those made rich through the capitalist economy with its international ramifications. Ostensibly the heads of private organizations, capitalists can dictate to governments and govern dictators. Britain is a traditional home of this international class of power. Thatcher's so-called resolution entailed little more than pushing at a series of open doors; the bulldozer had power-assisted steering. The small, intemperate grocer's daughter was the answer to the prayer of the mighty operating from their glass tower blocks at a barge-pole's length from the ballot box. When she spoke her 'common sense', her words were what they wanted to hear and her voice was amplified by the clarion of a right-wing press, the same press that derided Labour leaders, trade unionists, feminists and so on. It was the mighty thermal currents of hegemony, rather than her resolution, which enabled her New Right balloon to soar.

Any idea that a Labour prime minister could act with the same 'resolution' to reverse the momentum of the anti-state bandwagon or eradicate the individualist culture is fantasy. There can be no alternative to the approach of the great Roman, Quintus Fabius Maximus Verrucosus, nicknamed *Cunctator* (delayer). Although not a cry to set the heart beating faster, stealthy Fabian gradualism saved Rome by wearing down the mighty Hannibal and is the only way to wear down the forces of individualism. Indeed, a Fabian Pamphlet goes so far as to argue that for socialists to 'simply oppose individualism in all its guises' would be 'to fall into a trap' (Barry 1989). The task of realizing the communal instinct and building the communal state is truly a Sisyphean one. Indeed, Sisyphus, doomed in Hades for ever to push a large boulder up a hill from where it would only descend to the bottom again, may well have preferred his task to that of Neil Kinnock. Restoring the ideals of social democracy cannot be a project only for the left; by definition it requires the broad consensus that so incensed Thatcher. The notion of the community cannot be pursued by a class-based policy.

The Sisyphean nature of the task was revealed in its full magnitude in the general election of 1992, when the anti-tax, individualist political culture spoke more loudly than ever it had in the Thatcher years. The prisoners in the polling booths faced their dilemma in fear. With all the economic indicators singing the requiem to an economy in the deepest recession since the Second World War, they feared unemployment, rising interest rates and house repossessions, but most of all they feared the tax implications of the policies for regeneration. They opted to cling to the Conservative nurse for fear of finding something even worse in a collectivist approach. As always the Conservative cause was mightily assisted by the tabloid press, where 'rabid anti-Labour coverage was wound up to fever pitch' (Will Hutton in *The Guardian*, 11 April 1992). *The Sun* was not reticent about its role: 'IT'S THE SUN WOT WON IT' proclaimed its post-election headline, and for once few on the centre-left were inclined to challenge the veracity of the judgement. The election was a very British affair; it ignored the environment (the winning party saw litter as the main problem), Europe and indeed the world. Herein lies the greatest tragedy of all.

Global tragedy

This essay may seem an incestuous exercise. Almost obscenely it has ignored the fact that we live in a world where one half grows fat while the other starves; the strong nations exploit the weak with impunity. However, both areas of concern are part of the same; a nation which denies the existence of society at home will not be one to recognize a global responsibility. Indeed, Britain trails in its record on third world aid, as does the US, the 'special partner' worshipping at the same altar of individualism. If the price is right, they are generous in the world arms bazaar, but in the world soup kitchen they remain parsimonious. The stockpile of arms throughout the world remains horrifyingly high; the equivalent of 114,000 Hiroshima bombs wait silently in the silos (Popper 1991) and the imbalance of wealth raises envy and greed to the critical mass for a final holocaust. Moreover, the failure of communism removes what was once a source of hope for the destitute populations, and the grim forewarnings of Marx, and indeed Malthus, become more insistent than ever.

In addition, the probability of the suicide of the entire human species through insane environmental vandalism grows greater. Environmental systems are essentially global in operation (Johnston 1992). Careless of the vanities of race, territory and nationalistic competition, they can only be handled through a global spirit of community (or a Hobbesian superstate Leviathan). Without this, the war of all against all, enlarged to monstrous proportions, must precipitate global tragedy in which a diseased planet, no longer able to sustain life, must spin towards eternity in a black void.

Plato claimed famously to be a citizen not of Athens but of the world. The need for a future predicated upon a communal culture goes beyond national economic recovery, the moral claims of egalitarians, the cry for justice by socialists, or even the quest for the good life. It is linked to the sustainability of life on the planet; in a world which believes only the fittest should survive, none will survive.

REFERENCES

Almond, G. A. and Verba, S. (1963) *The Civic Culture*. Princeton, NJ, Princeton University Press.

Alt, J. E. (1979) *The Politics of Economic Decline: Economic Management and Political Behaviour in Britain Since 1964*. Cambridge, Cambridge University Press.

Arblaster, A. (1977) 'Anthony Crosland: Labour's last revisionist', *Political Quarterly*, 48, 416–28.

Arrow, K. (1951) *Social Choice and Individual Values*. New York, John Wiley and Sons.

Auster, R. D. and Silver, M. (1979) *The State as a Firm: Economic Forces in Political Development*. The Hague, Martinus Nijhoff.

Bagehot, W. (1963) (first published 1867) *The English Constitution* (with an introduction by A. Crosland). London, Fontana.

Balogh, T. (1968) 'The apotheosis of the dilettante: the establishment of mandarins', in H. Thomas (ed.) *Crisis in the Civil Service*. London, Anthony Blond.

Barratt Brown, M. (1991) *European Union: Fortress or Democracy*. Nottingham, Spokesman.

Barry, B. (1989) *Does Society Exist? The Case for Socialism*. London, Fabian Society.

Beer, S. H. (1982) *Britain Against Itself: The Political Contradictions of Collectivism*. London, Faber.

Bell, D. (1960) *The End of Ideology*. Glencoe, IL, Free Press.

Bentham, J. (1970) (first published 1789) *An Introduction to the Principles of Morals and Legislation* (edited by J. H. Burns and H. L. A. Hart). London, Athlone Press.

Bentley, A. F. (1967) (first published 1908) *The Process of Government*. Cambridge, MA, Harvard University Press.

Benyon, J. (1989) 'Ten years of Thatcherism', *Social Studies Review*, 4, 170–8.

Berlin, I. (1970) 'Two concepts of liberty', in I. Berlin *Four Essays on Liberty*. Oxford, Oxford University Press.

Bertalanffy, L. von (1956) 'General system theory', *General Systems*, 1, 1–10.

Beveridge, W. (chairman) (1942) *Social Insurance and Allied Services* (Cmd 6404). London, HMSO.

Beveridge, W. (1944) *Full Employment in a Free Society*. London, Allen and Unwin.

Beveridge, W. (1945) *Why I am a Liberal?* London, Herbert Jenkins.

Black, D. (chairman) (1980) *Inequalities in Health*. London, Department of Health and Social Security.

Boddy, M. and Fudge, C. (1984) *Local Socialism?* Basingstoke, Macmillan.

Boulding, K.E. (1973) *The Economy of Love and Fear*. Belmont, CA, Wadsworth.

Boyle, A. (1979) *The Climate of Treason*. London, Hutchinson.

Brittan, S. (1988) *A Restatement of Economic Liberalism*. Basingstoke, Macmillan.

Buchanan, J.M. (1962) 'Marginal notes on reading political philosophy', in J.M. Buchanan and G. Tullock *The Calculus of Consent*. Ann Arbor, MI, University of Michigan Press.

Buchanan, J.M. and Tullock, G. (1962) *The Calculus of Consent*. Ann Arbour, MI, University of Michigan Press.

Burnham, J. (1942) *The Managerial Revolution*. London, Putnam.

Cairncross, A. (1985) *Years of Recovery: British Economic Policy, 1945-51*. London, Methuen.

Church of England (1985) *Faith in the City: Report of the Archbishop of Canterbury's Commission on Urban Priority Areas*. London, Christian Action.

Coase, R.H. (1937) 'The nature of the firm', *Economica*, November.

Cornford, F.M. (ed.) (1941) *The Republic of Plato*. Oxford, Clarendon Press.

Crick, B. (1964) *In Defence of Politics*. Harmondsworth, Penguin.

Crick, B. (1987) *Socialism*. Milton Keynes, Open University Press.

Crosland, C.A.R. (1956) *The Future of Socialism*. London, Jonathan Cape.

Currie, R. (1979) *Industrial Politics*. Oxford, Oxford University Press.

Dahl, R.A. (1956) *A Preface to Democratic Theory*. Chicago, University of Chicago Press.

Demsetz, H. (1967) 'Toward a theory of property rights', *American Economic Review*, 57(2), 347-59.

Deutsch, K.W. (1964) *The Nerves of Government*. Glencoe, IL, Free Press.

Dore, R. (1986) 'Industrial policy and how the Japanese do it', *Catalyst*, Spring, 45-58.

Downs, A. (1957) *An Economic Theory of Democracy*. New York, Harper and Row.

Dunsire, A. (1973) *Administration: The Word and the Science*. London, Martin Robertson.

Dworkin, R. (1984) 'Liberalism', in M. Sandel (ed.) *Liberalism and its Critics*. Oxford, Basil Blackwell.

Easton, D. (1953) *The Political System*. New York, Knopf.

Eccleshall, R. (1986) *British Liberalism*. Harlow, Longman.

Elster, J. (1983) *Sour Grapes*. Cambridge, Cambridge University Press.

Esping-Andersen, G. (1985) *Politics Against Markets*. Princeton, Princeton University Press.

Field, F. (1982) *Poverty and Politics*. London, Heinemann.

Fox, A. (1985) *History and Heritage: The Social Origins of the British Industrial Relations System*. London, Allen and Unwin.

Frazer, J.G. (1925) *The Golden Bough* (abridged edition). London, Macmillan.

Friedman, D. (1973) *The Machinery of Freedom*. New York, Harper and Row.

Friedman, M. (1962) *Capitalism and Freedom*. Chicago, University of Chicago Press.

Friedman, M. and Friedman, R. (1980) *Free to Choose*. Harmondsworth, Penguin.

Fulton, Lord (chairman) (1968) *The Civil Service, Vol. 1: Report of the Committee* (Cmnd 3638). London, HMSO.

Galbraith, J.K. (1958) *The Affluent Society*. London, Hamish Hamilton.

Galbraith, J.K. (1977) *The Age of Uncertainty*. London, British Broadcasting Corporation.

Gamble, A. (1981) *An Introduction to Modern Social and Political Thought*. Basingstoke, Macmillan.

Gamble, A. (1985) *Britain in Decline*. Basingstoke, Macmillan.

Gamble, A. (1988) *The Economy and the Strong State*. Basingstoke, Macmillan.

Gewith, A. (1981) 'The basis and content of human rights', in J. Roland Pennock and J.W. Chapman (eds) *Human Rights*. London, New York University Press.

Goodin, R.E. (1982) 'Freedom and the welfare state: theoretical foundations', *Journal of Social Policy*, 11, 149–76.

Gould, B. (1985) *Socialism and Freedom*. Basingstoke, Macmillan.

Gramsci, A. (1971) *Selections from Prison Notebooks*. London, Lawrence and Wishart.

Green, T.H. and Grose, T.H. (eds) (1882) *Essays Moral, Political and Literary*. London, Longmans, Green and Co.

Greenleaf, W.H. (1983) *The British Political Tradition, Vol. 1: The Rise of Collectivism*. London, Methuen.

Hall, S. (1979) 'The great moving right show', *Marxism Today*, January.

Hall, S. (1980) 'Popular democratic versus authoritarian populism', in A. Hunt (ed.) *Marxism and Democracy*. London, Lawrence and Wishart.

Hall, S. (1984) 'The state in question', in G. McLennan, D. Held and S. Hall *The Idea of the Modern State*. Milton Keynes, Open University Press.

Hall, S. (1991) 'And not a shot fired', *Marxism Today*, December, 10–15.

Halsey, A.H. (1978) *Change in British Society*. Oxford, Oxford University Press.

Halsey, A.H., Heath, A.F. and Ridge, J.M. (1980) *Origins and Destination: Family, Class and Education in Modern Britain*. Oxford, Clarendon Press.

Hardach, K. (1980) *The Political Economy of Germany in the Twentieth Century*. Berkeley, CA, University of California Press.

Hardin, G. (1968) 'The tragedy of the commons', *Science*, 162, 1243–8.

Harris, D. (1987) *Justifying State Welfare: The New Right Versus the Old Left*. Oxford, Basil Blackwell.

Harris, R. and Seldon, A. (1979) *Over-ruled on Welfare*. London, Institute of Economic Affairs.

Hattersley, R. (1987) *Choose Freedom: The Future of Democratic Socialism*. Harmondsworth, Penguin.

Hayek, F.A. (1982) *Law, Legislation and Liberty*. London, Routledge and Kegan Paul.

Heald, D. (1983) *Public Expenditure*. Oxford, Martin Robertson.

Heclo, H. and Wildavsky, A. (1974) *The Private Government of Public Money*. London, Macmillan.

Hegel, F. (1942) (first published 1821) *The Philosophy of Right* (translated with notes by T.M. Knox). Oxford, Clarendon Press.

Hennessy, P. (1989) *Whitehall*. London, Fontana.

Himmelweit, H., Humphreys, P. and Jaeger, M. (1985) *How Voters Decide*. Milton Keynes, Open University Press.

Hindess, B. (1987) *Freedom, Equality and the Market*. London, Tavistock.

Hindess, B. and Hirst, P.Q. (1983) 'Labour's crisis', *New Society*, 29 September.

Hirsch, F. (1976) *The Social Limits to Growth*. Cambridge, MA, Harvard University Press.

Hirschman, A.O. (1970) *Exit, Voice and Loyalty: Responses to Decline in Firms, Organisations and States*. Cambridge, MA, Harvard University Press.

Hobbes, T. (1839) 'Elements of philosophy: the first section concerning the body', in W. Molesworth (ed.) *The English Works of Thomas Hobbes, Vol. 1*. London, Bohn.

Hobbes, T. (1968) (first published 1651) *Leviathan* (edited by C.B. Macpherson). Harmondsworth, Penguin.

Hodgson, G. (1984) *The Democratic Economy*. Harmondsworth, Penguin.

Hoskyns, Sir J. (1984) 'Conservatism is not enough', *Political Quarterly*, 55, 3–16.

Hutton, W. (1986) *The Revolution that Never Was*. London, Longman.

Jenkins, K., Caines, K. and Jackson, A. (1988) *Improving Management in Government: The Next Steps*. London, HMSO (known as the Ibbs Report).

Jessop, B., Bonnett, K., Bromley, S. and Long, T. (1988) *Thatcherism*. Oxford, Polity.

Johnson, C. (1982) *MITI and the Japanese Miracle: The Growth of Industrial Policy, 1925-1975*. Stanford, CA, Stanford University Press.

Johnston, R. (1992) 'Laws, states and super-states: international law and the environment', *Applied Geography*, 12.

Jowell, R., Brook, L. and Taylor, B. (1991) *British Social Attitudes*. Dartmouth, Dartmouth Publishing Company.

Kant, I. (1948) *The Moral Law* (translated by H.J. Paton). London, Hutchinson.

Kaufman, H. (1976) *Are Government Institutions Immortal?* Washington, DC, Brookings Institution.

Keynes, J.M. (1919) *The Economic Consequences of the Peace*. London, Macmillan.

Keynes, J.M. (1936) *The General Theory of Employment, Interest and Money*. London, Macmillan.

Kingdom, J. (1991) *Local Government and Politics in Britain*. Hemel Hempstead, Philip Allan.

Klein, R. (1989) *Politics of the NHS* (2nd edn). Harlow, Longman.

Knightly, P. (1968) *The Second Oldest Profession: The Spy as Bureaucrat, Fantasist and Whore*. London, André Deutsch.

Kohn, H. (1955) *Nationalism*. New York, Van Nostrand.

Kymlicka, W. (1989) *Liberalism, Community and Culture*. Oxford, Clarendon Press.

Labour Party (1989) *Meet the Challenge, Make the Change*. London, Labour Party.

Lamprecht, S.P. (ed.) (1949) *De Cive; or the Citizen*. New York, Appleton-Century-Crofts.

Land, H. and Rose, H. (1985) 'Compulsory altruism for some or an altruistic society for all', in P. Bean, J. Ferris and D. Whynes (eds) *In Defence of Welfare*. London, Tavistock.

Laver, M. (1986) 'Public, private and common in outer space: *res extra commercium* or *res communis humanitatis* beyond the high frontier?', *Political Studies*, 34, 359–73.

Le Grand, J. (1982) *The Strategy of Equality*. London, Allen and Unwin.

Lehmbruch, G. and Schmitter, P. (eds) (1982) *Patterns of Corporatist Policy-Making*. London, Sage.

Lindblom, C.E. (1977) *Politics and Markets: The World's Political-Economic Systems*. New York, Basic Books.

Lively, J. (1975) *Democracy*. Oxford, Basil Blackwell.

Locke, J. (1988) (first published 1690) *Two Treatises of Government* (edited by P. Laslett). Cambridge, Cambridge University Press.

Macmillan, H. (1938) *The Middle Way: A Study of the Problem of Economic and Social Progress in a Free and Democratic Society*. London, Macmillan.

Macpherson, C.B. (1962) *The Political Theory of Possessive Individualism*. Oxford, Oxford University Press.

Magaziner, I.C. and Hout, T.M. (1980) *Japanese Industrial Policy*. London, Policy Studies Institute.

Mair, L. (1962) *Primitive Government*. Harmondsworth, Penguin.

Marcuse, H. (1964) *One Dimensional Man*. London, Routledge and Kegan Paul.

Marini, F. (ed.) (1973) *Towards a New Public Administration*. Lexington, Lexington Books.

Marquand, D. (1988) *The Unprincipled Society*. London, Fontana.

Marshall, T.H. (1950) *Citizenship and Social Class and Other Essays*. Cambridge, Cambridge University Press.

Marwick, A. (1982) *British Society Since 1945*. Harmondsworth, Penguin.

Marx, K. (1930) (first published 1867) *Capital* (translated from the 4th German edition by E. and C. Paul). London, Dent.

Middlemas, K. (1979) *Politics in Industrial Society*. London, André Deutsch.

Miliband, R. (1961) *Parliamentary Socialism*. London, Merlin.

Miliband, R. (1984) *Capitalist Democracy in Britain*. Oxford, Oxford University Press.

Mill, J. S. (1848) *Principles of Political Economy*. London, J. W. Parker.

Mill, J. S. (1859) *On Liberty*. London, J. W. Parker.

Milne, A. (1988) *DG: Memoirs of a British Broadcaster*. London, Hodder and Stoughton.

Mitchell, W. C. (1969) 'The shape of things to come', in S. M. Lipset (ed.) *Politics and the Social Sciences*. New York, Oxford University Press.

Murray, R. (1991) 'The state after Henry', *Marxism Today*, May, 22–7.

Niskanen, W. A. (1971) *Bureaucracy and Representative Government*. Chicago, Aldine Atherton.

Nozick, R. (1974) *Anarchy, State and Utopia*. Oxford, Basil Blackwell.

O'Connor, J. (1973) *The Fiscal Crisis of the State*. New York, St Martin's Press.

Olson, M. (1968) *The Logic of Collective Action*. New York, Schocken.

Olson, M. (1982) *The Rise and Decline of Nations*. New Haven, Yale University Press.

Pahl, R. (1975) *Whose City?* Harmondsworth, Penguin.

Paine, T. (1791) *The Rights of Man*. London, J. Johnson.

Peterson, W. E. and Thomas, A. (eds) (1986) *The Future of Social Democracy*. Oxford, Oxford University Press.

Piachaud, D. (1991) 'Revitalising social policy', *Political Quarterly*, 62(2), 204–24.

Plant, R., Lesser, H. and Taylor-Gooby, P. (1980) *Political Philosophy and Social Welfare*. London, Routledge and Kegan Paul.

Poggi, G. (1978) *The Development of the Modern State*. London, Hutchinson.

Polanyi, K. (1957) *The Great Transformation*. New York, Rinehart.

Ponting, C. (1986) *Whitehall: Tragedy and Farce*. London, Hamish Hamilton.

Popper, K. (1991) 'Grave new world', *Marxism Today*, December, 42.

Poulantzas, N. (1978) *State, Power, Socialism* (translated by Patrick Camiller). London, New Left Books.

Ranson, S. and Stewart, J. (1989) 'Citizenship and government: the challenge for management in the public domain', *Political Studies*, 37, 5–24.

Rawls, J. (1973) *A Theory of Justice*. Oxford, Oxford University Press.

Raz, J. (1986) *The Morality of Freedom*. Oxford, Oxford University Press.

Rothbard, M. (1978) *For a New Liberty: The Libertarian Manifesto*. New York, Collier Books.

Rousseau, J. J. (1913) (first published 1762) *The Social Contract*. London, Dent.

Rousseau, J. J. (1953) *The Confessions of Jean-Jacques Rousseau* (translated and with introduction by J. M. Cohen). Harmondsworth, Penguin.

Sandel, M. (ed.) (1984) *Liberalism and its Critics*. Oxford, Basil Blackwell.

Schumpeter, J. A. (1976) (first published in Britain in 1943) *Capitalism, Socialism and Democracy*. London, Allen and Unwin.

Scott, J. (1991) *Who Rules Britain?* Oxford, Polity.

Shonfield, A. (1965) *Modern Capitalism: The Changing Balance of Public and Private Power*. London, Oxford University Press.

Simhony, A. (1991) 'On forcing individuals to be free: T. H. Green's liberal theory of positive freedom', *Political Studies*, 39, 303–20.

Skinner, Q. (1978) *The Foundations of Modern Political Thought, Vol. 1*. Cambridge, Cambridge University Press.

Smith, A. (1976) (first published 1776) *An Enquiry Into the Nature and Causes of the Wealth of Nations*. Chicago, University of Chicago Press.

Spencer, H. (1865) *Social Statics*. New York, Appleton and Co.

Stanworth, P. and Giddens, A. (1974) *Elites and Power in British Society*. Cambridge, Cambridge University Press.

Stone, L. (1980) 'The results of the English revolutions of the seventeenth century', in J. G. A. Pocock (ed.) *The Three British Revolutions: 1641, 1688, 1776*. Princeton, NJ, Princeton University Press.

Sugden, R. (1981) *The Political Economy of Public Choice*. Oxford, Martin Robertson.

Tawney, R. H. (1931) *Equality*. London, Allen and Unwin.

Therborn, G. (1982) 'What does the ruling class do when it rules?', in A. Giddens and D. Held (eds) *Classes, Power and Conflict*. Basingstoke, Macmillan.

Thucydides (1954) *History of the Peloponnesian War* (translated and with an introduction by R. Warner). Harmondsworth, Penguin.

Thurrow, L. (1981) *The Zero-Sum Society: Distribution and the Possibilities for Economic Change*. Harmondsworth, Penguin.

Tiebout, C. (1956) 'A pure theory of local expenditures', *Journal of Political Economy*, 64, 416–24.

Titmuss, R. (1970) *The Gift Relationship*. London, Allen and Unwin.

Tocqueville, A. de (1971) (first published 1856) *The Ancien Régime and the French Revolution* (translated by S. Gilbert). London, Fontana.

Townsend, P. (1979) *Poverty in the United Kingdom*. Harmondsworth, Penguin.

Tullock, G. (1965) *The Politics of Bureaucracy*. Washington, DC, Public Affairs Press.

Tullock, G. (1976) *The Vote Motive: An Essay in the Economics of Politics, with Applications to the British Economy*. London, Institute of Economic Affairs.

Vaizey, J. (1983) *In Breach of Promise*. London, Weidenfeld and Nicolson.

Vaughan, C. (ed.) (1962) *Political Writings of Jean-Jacques Rousseau*. Oxford, Basil Blackwell.

Veblen, T. (1970) (first published in Britain 1925) *The Theory of the Leisure Class*. London, Allen and Unwin.

Waldo, D. (ed.) (1971) *Public Administration in a Time of Turbulence*. Scranton, Chandler.

Walvin, J. (1984) *Passage to Britain*. Harmondsworth, Penguin.

Wasserstrom, R. (1964) 'Rights, human rights and racial discrimination', *Journal of Philosophy*, LXI, 628–41.

Weale, A. (1990) 'Can *Homo economicus* have a political theory?', *Political Studies*, 38, 512–25.

Weber, M. (1961) *General Economic History*. New York, Collier Books.

Weiner, N. (1965) *Cybernetics*. Cambridge, MA, MIT Press.

Widdicombe, D. (1986) *The Conduct of Local Authority Business: Report of the Committee of Inquiry* (Cmnd 9797). London, HMSO.

Wilkinson, R. G. (1991) 'Inequality is bad for your health', *The Guardian*, 12 June.

Young, H. (1990) *One of Us*. London, Pan.

INDEX